Achieving a low-carbon household: a guide for the better off

Bob Whitmarsh

Achieving a low-carbon household: a guide for the better off

The information and suggestions provided in this book have been included in good faith to assist the reader. The author offers no warranties or representations in respect of their fitness for a particular purpose nor does he accept liability for any loss or damage arising from their use. The author makes no representation, express or implied, with regard to the accuracy of information contained in this book nor does he accept any legal responsibility or liability for any errors or omissions in the text. The author does not intend to provide a professional service and if such a service is required the reader should seek professional advice.

First printing: February 2017

Front cover credits: images from
https://pixabay.com/en/high-speed-train-railway-ice-train-146498/ and
http://www.freepik.com/free-photo/house-with-a-solar-panel-on-the-roof_959160.htm#term=solar panel&page=2&position=13 (Designed by D3images - Freepik.com)

Front cover design and photos by the author

ISBN 978-1542849951

To my oceanographic colleagues, past and present, who work on the high seas, often in difficult conditions, to make many of the measurements that underpin our understanding of climate science, and the families that they leave behind, often for weeks at a time.

A coal-burning power station

CONTENTS

PREFACE

What this book is about

For some years I have been recording the energy, mainly electricity and gas but also car fuel, used by our household. I was astonished one day to realise that over some nine years we had cut our consumption of gas and reduced our car miles by over 40 per cent. We had not succeeded as well with electricity consumption because it had barely reduced over the same period. But even more encouraging was that our total greenhouse gas emissions, electricity included, had been cut by over 60 per cent.[1] And of course it is greenhouse gas emissions produced by human activities which are known to be causing global warming and climate change, and which everyone should seek to reduce on a personal level.

How was this done? The answer lies in some changes in our behaviour or lifestyle, but also in investing in a range of modifications to our house and buying a car which emitted less carbon dioxide per kilometre. Together these had the effect of reducing our emissions. Admittedly I was fortunate in that during this period I was retired with a good pension and our mortgage had been paid off. In that sense my wife and I could be classed among the financially better off. But, as I shall seek to show, there are many people in the UK who are also 'better off' and who, if they wished or were given some encouragement, could make similar savings. Indeed, it is well known that on average the carbon footprint, which is a measure of the annual emissions attributable to an individual, of the better off is much greater than that of many of those less financially fortunate. So it is clear that for the UK, or for any other developed country, to drastically reduce its carbon emissions[2] one part of the solution should be for the better off to step up to the plate and do their significant bit.

I would emphasise that, as explained later, the changes we made had minimal effects on our lifestyle. I shall show that, as an example, if the richest tenth of UK households were to reduce their emissions by half, the next two richest tenths of households reduce their emissions by 30 and 20 per cent, respectively, and the rest, bar the poorest tenth, each reduce their emissions by 10 per cent that would save 20 per cent of the UK's emissions by households (or 12 per cent of all the UK's emissions). It is worth recognising that, in comparison with the vast majority of the world's population, those of us in developed countries live lives of relative luxury.

Exactly who can be defined as 'better off'? Clearly it depends on income and particularly on disposable income. Anyone who has money left over at the end of the week or month should be in a position to put some of it away to spend on making their home more energy efficient and to help them lead a less carbon-emitting lifestyle. The UK Office of National Statistics estimates that on average, since early 2013, households have more often been in a position to save money than not.[3] Other people may also have substantial incomes yet have next to nothing left over at the end of the week or month. Perhaps they should be reviewing their outgoings in order to make some savings to invest in the same way. There is no doubt that climate change which we, in developed countries, have helped and are helping to drive by our high-carbon-emitting lifestyles, is here to stay for a long time. In any event many changes in behaviour or lifestyle are cost-free and can help you save money too. Even some of the energy-saving suggestions made here that involve some initial expenditure will eventually lead to net financial savings as well.

My intention in writing this book is to encourage individuals and households, particularly the better off, to take greater responsibility for the emissions from their homes and lifestyles. I give many examples of how individuals and households can contribute in a limited, but together substantial, way to mitigate climate change. There are many things we can do that do not result in a less comfortable lifestyle, just in a more intelligent one. The damaging aspects of climate change are well known. They include extreme weather events, which today feature so frequently in the news, rising sea levels and other unpleasant and socially disruptive manifestations of this phenomenon.

It is a cop out for those of us who are better off to wait for government, whether local or national, to tell us what to do and even to pay for or subsidise what can be done at a personal level. The technical solutions to reducing carbon emissions are obvious but their implementation is held back by politics and by those with a vested interest in maintaining business as usual. Given the urgency with which climate change needs to be addressed the time for action is now.

An overview of the chapters

Chapters 1 and 2 deal with climate change and the global demand for energy. Both chapters present reasons, from two different viewpoints, for swiftly abandoning humanity's current dependence on fossil fuels. Chapter 3 explores the contribution that personal carbon emissions make to climate change on both global and national (UK) scales. This provides the premise on which the rest of the book is built, which is that individuals and households can have a substantial influence on present and future carbon emissions and therefore on climate change. The next five chapters are very practical in that they describe how one can measure one's own energy use from electricity, gas and getting about, including travelling on holiday. These chapters also explain the relationships between energy use and carbon emissions. Chapter 9 gives individual examples of how some households have managed to reduce their carbon emissions either by retrofitting their homes to varying degrees or by building a new home to a high standard. Chapter 10 addresses some of the economic aspects of how individuals and households may reduce their carbon emissions. In particular it suggests how to avoid self-defeating actions, when spending the money accumulated from saving energy, that will cause further carbon emissions. Finally Chapter 11 presents climate change in the wider context of other current global problems. It urges the reader to face up to deciding how they will act to reduce their emissions and how they can work with others to achieve this aim.

Sources consulted

Sources I consulted are referenced in the text and listed by chapter under Notes and References at the end of the book. Many are accessible as web pages or as downloadable reports, others are published books and articles in magazines and a few are articles in scientific journals.

CHAPTER 1: THE CHANGING CLIMATE

"Yet the science is crystal clear. We have a climate and energy crisis, an emergency" James Hansen, April 2016[4]

How the world is warming[5]

The Sun warms the Earth. Yet, if it weren't for the clouds of water vapour largely enshrouding the Earth, it is estimated that the average surface temperature would be as low as -18°C, whereas it is in fact +15°C. Incoming ultraviolet radiation from the Sun, the radiation which can cause sunburn if you lie in the Sun too long, is absorbed by the Earth and re-radiated as infrared radiation, the sort of radiation that your TV controller uses. This outgoing infrared radiation interacts with water vapour and other greenhouse gases in the atmosphere trapping heat. The water vapour maintains an almost constant presence; if the atmosphere becomes saturated with water vapour then rain or snow will fall.[6] The other principal greenhouse gases are carbon dioxide (CO_2),[7] methane and nitrous oxide, all of which exist in minute quantities. These gases have an effect on the atmosphere's temperature out of all proportion to their concentration. For example, there are only around 400 parts per million (ppm), or 0.04 per cent, of CO_2. The small amounts of these gases largely control how much of the outgoing infrared radiation is absorbed. If the amounts increase then the atmosphere warms up.

For millions of years the atmospheric concentration of greenhouse gases has stayed within limits determined by natural processes. The global climate has been more or less in an equilibrium state with a balance between the natural emissions of greenhouse gases, from volcanoes, wildfires, rotting vegetation and so on and their uptake by the natural sinks of the atmosphere, the ocean and living vegetation. Changes in global temperature have taken place only slowly.[8] On the other hand, mostly since the start of the industrial revolution in the mid-18th century, humanity has inadvertently acted to upset this equilibrium. Fossil fuels, first in the form of coal, and then as oil and natural gas, have been burnt in huge quantities and by doing so have added to the CO_2 in the atmosphere. Similarly there have been significant changes in land use, for example the planting of rice paddies to feed a growing population, and the rearing of huge numbers of cattle, both of which generate the powerful greenhouse gas methane, and the destruction of peat bogs and forests that normally store carbon, which also leads to the generation of CO_2.[9]

There is ample evidence that the amount of CO_2 in the atmosphere has increased by over 40 per cent since pre-industrial time. It has now passed 400 ppm and is actually increasing at a growing rate. At the same time the global temperature has steadily increased at an astounding rate of around 0.16°C per decade since 1970. 2016 was the warmest year since instrumental measurements began and global warming, relative to pre-industrial time, is approaching 1.1°C.[10] The current rate of warming is in line with the observed increase in atmospheric carbon dioxide and has been estimated to be at least nine times faster than anything that happened in the last 66 million years.[11]

The Intergovernmental Panel on Climate Change (IPCC) is a United Nations body which assesses the state of the climate every few years based on results published in peer-reviewed scientific journals. Hundreds of climate scientists and representatives of around 40 countries were involved in producing their Fifth Assessment reports in 2014 and 2015. The main result of the latest assessment is very clear. In 2014 the often cautious IPCC stated that man-made greenhouse gas emissions *"..are extremely likely* [i.e. 95-100 per cent certain] *to have been the dominant cause of the observed warming since the mid-20th century"*.[12]

This chapter explores some consequences of climate change which are the main reasons why mankind has to stop using fossil fuels, almost as soon as possible, to avoid the adverse effects of this phenomenon.

Extreme weather

So how bad is the situation and how concerned should we be that global warming is occurring? As mentioned above, warming is on the verge of reaching 1.1°C relative to pre-industrial time. This might seem like something to look forward to if large areas of the UK have winters with much less ice and snow and in years to come the south coast experiences Mediterranean temperatures. But there are far more serious downsides to this warming on local, regional and global scales. As the atmosphere warms up so the movements of the air become more energetic and clouds can hold more water vapour. Already we see many examples of the consequences of this around the globe in the form of extreme weather events such as storms and floods. Elsewhere there have been droughts and heat waves. Here are some examples.

In 1999 cyclone Odisha was the strongest ever recorded in the northern Indian Ocean; it caused the deaths of about 10,000 people. In 2013 typhoon Haiyan was one of the strongest tropical cyclones ever recorded; it killed at least 6,300 people in the Philippines alone. In February 2016 cyclone Winston, *"the most powerful storm on record"*, damaged the island of Fiji in the Southwest Pacific Ocean.[13] Odisha, Haiyan and Winston were all category 5 storms, the strongest on the Saffir-Simpson scale which is used to grade hurricane winds. Hurricane Katrina (New Orleans, 2005) and Superstorm Sandy (New York, 2012) which caused immense damage in the USA and around 2,000 deaths, mostly in New Orleans, were weaker category 3 storms.

In Europe, floods are of special concern. Between 1980 and 2010, 37 European countries registered a total of 3,563 floods. In some countries the proportion of the population living in flood plains is substantial (11 per cent in Italy, 18 per cent in Hungary).[14] The UK experienced severe flooding in Somerset in 2013/2014 and in Cumbria in 2015/2016. Heavy monsoon floods in 2010 in the Indus river basin in Pakistan caused a death toll of close to 2,000 people and are said to have directly affected about 20 million people.

A heat wave in France in 2003 led to the deaths of almost 15,000, mostly elderly, people. In California a prolonged drought that had lasted over four years led to the declaration of a state of emergency in January 2015. In Australia parts of Queensland and Victoria have suffered a 40-month 'rainfall deficiency' since October 2012. Large parts of south-west Australia and the state of Victoria have experienced abnormally dry condition for 16 years.[15] Homes in both California and Australia have been destroyed by wildfires.

Climate scientists are now able to test to what extent some particular extreme weather events can be attributed to man-made climate change. For instance, *"Human influence increased … the risk of heavy precipitation in southern England"* at the time of the floods in 2012/2013.[16] Preliminary results suggest that, regarding the floods in December 2015 in north-west England, *"the role of human influence on climate was as large or larger than the influence of these* [natural] *patterns of ocean variability, but that random and unpredictable atmospheric weather noise played an important role as well."* and that *"climate change increased the odds of the exceptionally high rainfall by 50-75%."*[17]

The frequency, and even the severity, of extreme weather events seem to be increasing. More disturbing is that, as global warming continues, what passes for extreme weather today may become the norm in a few decades to come. Even five years ago a report for Munich RE, the worldwide insurance and reinsurance company, found that since 1980 there had been a threefold

8

increase in the annual frequency of weather events worldwide that had caused losses. These losses have increased at a rate equivalent to about US$2.7 billion per year.[18]

Rising sea level

Another insidious result of global warming is rising sea level. As the ice sheets of Greenland and onshore Antarctica melt, and glaciers elsewhere do likewise, extra water is added to the ocean. The thermal expansion of the warming oceans also contributes to sea level rise to about the same extent. Oceanographers have found that globally the oceans have been on a warming trend since 1958. Since the year 2000 measurements in the top two thousand metres of the ocean by almost four thousand free-floating buoys worldwide show that this warming trend has continued unchecked.[19] Sea level is estimated to rise by up to one metre by the end of this century[20] but there are several uncertainties in this estimate, such as the rates of melting in Greenland and Antarctica and changes in the strength of some ocean currents. Regionally the rise could be more or less. A rise in sea level of up to two metres by the end of this century, corresponding to a global temperature increase of 4°C or more, will likely put 187 million people at risk of displacement.[21] At the end of the 20th century around 2.5 million people in the UK, including 1 million in London, lived at elevations within five metres of mean sea level.[22] The IPCC has noted that many small island states (Marshall Islands, Kiribati, Tuvalu, Tonga, the Federated States of Micronesia, and the Cook Islands in the Pacific Ocean), Antigua and Nevis (in the Caribbean Sea), and the Maldives (in the Indian Ocean) are at risk of disappearing beneath the waves.[23] Scientists recently reported that in the Solomon Islands in the western Pacific five vegetated reef islands have disappeared beneath the waves since 1947 and six more have suffered substantial losses in area.[24]

9

Geologists have shown that 125,000 years ago, when the temperature was also 1°C warmer than pre-industrial times, sea level was six to nine metres higher than today. 125,000 years ago the warming was driven by natural forces, primarily changes in the Earth's orbit around the Sun, whereas today we know that the growing man-made emissions of greenhouse gases are the driving force. However in the long term the response of the Earth system to this atmospheric warming will be the same whatever the cause. So we may expect sea level to have risen by six to nine metres several centuries from now, even if warming is halted this century, because the Earth system takes a long time to reach a new equilibrium state.[25]

North Atlantic currents

It is well known that the climate of western Europe is tempered by the warm currents of the Gulf Stream. For example, places in North America at the same latitude as the UK experience much more severe winters. In fact the Gulf Stream, composed of warm surface waters that drift north-eastwards and eastwards from the Gulf of Mexico and Caribbean region and give up their heat to westerly winds, is only one part of a much larger, so-called conveyor-belt system of moving water masses in the North Atlantic Ocean and globally. Put very simply, the warm water crossing the North Atlantic eventually cools and sinks and returns southwards as a deep cold current. This system of currents has been monitored by oceanographers between the Bahamas and NW Africa since 2004. They have found that although the flow does vary considerably with the seasons and from year to year there has been a steady decline in the strength of the flow.[26]

This decline, which might eventually produce an unwelcome cooling influence on Europe's climate, is the subject of continuing research. It might be caused by global warming melting Greenland ice to form a cold, but less dense, freshwater layer at the top of

10

the ocean which prevents the cold water from sinking and providing the deep return current described above.[27] This idea provides yet one more argument, specific to the climate of Europe, for reducing global greenhouse gas emissions. On the other hand there is a suggestion that this decline in North Atlantic flows follows an intensification in circulation over the preceding decade. Thus, the weakening circulation in the past 12 years or so could well be part of a longer-term, decadal-scale natural variability rather than having been induced by global warming.[28]

Health hazards

Climate change is also predicted to be the biggest threat to global health in the 21st century. In 2009 a large group of scientists based at University College, London completed a major study of the health effects of climate change. They described how changing patterns of disease, insecurity in supplies of water and food, vulnerable shelter and human settlements, extreme climatic events, and population growth and migration would all affect health. They said that although vector-borne diseases will expand their reach, and death tolls will increase because of heatwaves, especially among elderly people, the indirect effects of climate change on water supply, food security, and extreme climatic events are likely to have the greatest impact.[29] The authors noted that *"Climate change will have its greatest effect on those who have the least access to the world's resources and who have contributed least to its cause."*

A similar major study of the impact of climate change on the health of its citizens was conducted by USA government agencies which reported in 2016.[30] It acknowledged that the USA has already experienced *"climate-related increases in our exposure to elevated temperatures; more frequent, severe, or longer-lasting extreme events; degraded air quality; diseases transmitted through food, water, and disease vectors (such as ticks and*

11

mosquitoes); and stresses to our mental health and well-being." and these would get worse. The report notes that on balance any potential health benefits from a warming climate, such as fewer cold-related deaths, will be exceeded by negative impacts. Again, as noted in the previous paragraph, *"some populations are disproportionately vulnerable, including those with low income, some communities of color, immigrant groups (including those with limited English proficiency), Indigenous peoples, children and pregnant women, older adults, vulnerable occupational groups, persons with disabilities, and persons with preexisting or chronic medical conditions."*

One example of the spread of a disease carried by mosquitoes, and possibly accentuated by global warming, appeared in 2016. The Zika virus, which can damage the brain development of unborn babies, was first recognised in Uganda and has been identified in Central and South America, Mexico, and the Caribbean since 2015. It is now suspected that the virus has been transmitted locally in Miami-Dade County of Florida and in Puerto Rico.[31]

There are also concerns that the *Aedes albopictus* mosquito, which carries dengue fever, could lead to seasonal outbreaks of the disease in southern Europe where the mosquito is already established. At present there are no drugs or vaccines to combat this virus. Reports have shown that even small rises in temperature could allow the mosquito population to increase ten-fold. This is because as the temperature rises, the number of blood meals taken by the mosquito, and the number of times they lay eggs, increase.[32]

Here is another example, this time from a high latitude, of global warming affecting human health. In August 2016 in the Russian Arctic a boy died and 72 nomadic herders had to be treated in hospital as a result of anthrax infection. This followed an outbreak of anthrax among herds of reindeer. It is suspected that anthrax spores, which can survive in a frozen state for centuries, may have escaped into the air after the region had experienced unusually high temperatures which caused frozen animal remains to thaw out.[33]

One can only hope that the important and disquieting reports of the USA government agencies and others will cause at least some of those who question the reality of climate change to accept the situation that we face worldwide.

Nature danger

While climate change will undoubtedly affect the human race directly what will happen to the natural world and, consequently, to humans? Our species, *Homo sapiens,* is just one species among a multitude that makes up the global ecosystem. If we drastically disturb this system it will affect us as well as all the other species. Tony Juniper, the well known UK environmental campaigner and former director of Friends of the Earth, has written two books which explain in detail how we depend on the free services provided by nature. For example, we depend on the pollination of many crops and plants which is provided by insects.[34]

As the climate warms, albeit almost imperceptibly, insects respond by moving to habitats in which they are more comfortable. This means they migrate to higher and cooler altitudes or, in the northern hemisphere, northwards. Butterflies provide an excellent example of this. In its annual report on the *State of the UK's Butterflies 2015* Butterfly Conservation gives examples of several species which, since 1970, have extended their range northwards within England, and even into Scotland, most likely in response to climate change.

Of course, moving to higher altitudes is not always an option because the habitat in which the insect or plant already lives will be limited by the local topographic relief and in this case local extinction is highly likely. The coffee plant is a good example of this. Because the plant grows best in a certain range of temperatures the arrival of higher temperatures, long droughts punctuated by intense rainfall, more resilient pests and plant diseases - all of which are associated with climate change - have reduced coffee supplies dramatically in recent years.[35] How many of us realise that the wholesale price of coffee has actually quadrupled between 2002 and 2015?

The IPCC's 2014 Fifth Assessment Report, which I mentioned earlier, noted that many terrestrial, freshwater and marine species have shifted their geographic ranges and activities in response to climate change.[36] However, it is likely that some species will be unable to move fast enough to keep up with expected changes. It has been suggested that on average predicted changes in temperature will be more than 200,000 times faster than rates seen in past (natural) shifts in habitat.[37] For other species their preferred habitats are too fragmented for them to successfully migrate to an adjacent, more favourable location. For example, only two per cent of the eastern United States contains the connected green space needed for animals to find new homes.[38] Whether a species cannot move fast enough or its habitat is too fragmented the consequence will be at least the local disappearance of that species.

A more subtle effect is the gradual changes that have taken place in the dates when various species first appear in spring (a topic known as phenology). A recent major project with 31 authors studied over 10,000 time series from land and sea, all lasting at least 20 years, and related them to temperature and precipitation. The scientists found that *"Differences in phenological responses to climate change among species can desynchronise ecological interactions and thereby threaten ecosystem function."*[39] In essence this rather dry statement means that ecosystems can be upset because species that previously depended on each other to develop at the same time in spring can

14

now appear at times several days apart with potentially disruptive consequences. In a comment on this research one scientist provided the example of a moth that hatches from an egg laid on an oak tree and depends for its survival on timing its emergence with when the oak tree buds burst into leaf. But because the cues for the two events are determined by different physiological mechanisms, but both are influenced by changes in temperature, the moth's timing may no longer reliably match that of the oak tree and the moth will not survive.[40] Looking ahead to 2050 the authors of the main study predicted that some phenological events may be up to 15 days earlier than now with potentially grave consequences for the species involved.

Finally it is worth recalling that the climatic changes taking place today are at the very least nine times faster than what has happened naturally in the last 66 million years. We really have little inkling of the consequences for the natural world of the changes that mankind has already set in motion.

The risks of climate change

The risks of climate change are hard for many people to appreciate. Although, as I have described, climate change is already driving extreme weather events and the global rise in sea level, both of which present clear dangers today, not everyone has direct experience of these factors. Consequently the risks of climate change can seem geographically distant as well as something to be addressed in a not well determined future time. Unlike the risks of air pollution, certain diseases and traffic accidents, for example, to many of us the risks of climate change seem too insubstantial and distant in time and space to cause us to take action. Psychologically this may be reassuring yet it ignores the possibility of relatively rapid changes in the climate, which can occur past so-called tipping points, when the Earth system may lurch into a different and more threatening state. For example, the powerful greenhouse gas methane exists in large quantities beneath the relatively shallow waters surrounding the Arctic Ocean as ice-like compounds, called gas hydrates, in sediments under the sea-bed. Should these shallow seas warm, causing the sea-bed sediments to experience warming beyond some critical temperature, there could be a relatively rapid release of methane into the atmosphere with disastrous consequences for global warming. The release would be unstoppable because the resulting warming atmosphere would lead to even warmer waters and the even greater emissions of methane as the result of a positive or reinforcing feedback loop.

The World Economic Forum and others, in their Global risks report 2016, attempted an up to date summary of global risks. They considered that a *"failure of climate-change mitigation and adaptation"*, while not quite the most likely risk in the year ahead, would have the greatest global impact if it happened.[41] The most likely risks are seen to be large-scale involuntary migration of people and extreme weather events, both of which it has been argued are related to climate change.

Risk is sometimes presented as simply a function of the likelihood of an event and the magnitude of that event's impact. But other factors are involved such as the individual or collective perception of risk and hence how this perception will affect individual or collective behaviour. As climate change scientist Mike Hulme has written *"One of the reasons we disagree about climate change is because we evaluate risks differently"*.[42] Our perception of, and response to, the risk of climate change is a huge topic that has cultural, social and psychological ramifications but which I shall not explore further here. The topic is treated at greater length by Mike Hulme in his book.

Climate change deniers and sceptics

It is worth saying a few words here about climate change deniers and sceptics. Climate change deniers live in a world of their own which is not based on facts or rational argument. They also tend to be very vociferous and sometimes are inclined to use intemperate language (to put it mildly) about those that have opposing views. As Valerie Masson-Delmotte, Co-Chair of IPCC's Working Group 1, put it in an interview with Carbon Brief "*we have to acknowledge that not everyone is sensitive to facts. Beliefs, values and ideologies can be a big filter for perception of facts.*" [43] Because the media, and especially the BBC, like to present what they regard as balanced arguments in interviews, deniers get, or at least were given until the BBC changed their policy a year or two ago, undue exposure seemingly out of all proportion to their numbers. Not surprisingly this has provoked protests from certain quarters.[44]

Many climate change deniers are not actually experts on this topic at all; they may have backgrounds in economics, law, politics and other non-scientific fields. As I often argue, would you trust your garage mechanic to diagnose your illness or your financial adviser to fit your new boiler? Their arguments are also often based on a limited number of approaches. These are that climate change is a conspiracy and the science is not yet certain; they cherry pick facts or isolated errors in published results. Their arguments can also be logically fallacious or based on misrepresentation.[45] Of course, by its nature, science is never certain because it continually pushes at the frontiers of knowledge. Science also has to operate under the realisation that it is impossible to prove absolutely that any particular hypothesis is true; unexpected circumstances may always arise in future that show it is wrong. A valid scientific hypothesis can only be shown to be false, it can never be shown to be unequivocally true. The oft quoted example is the statement that 'all swans are white'.

Only when European explorers reached Australia and observed black swans was that hypothesis proved to be false.

People's attitudes and beliefs fall within a wide spectrum between deniers and climate scientists. In 2009 a survey of over ten thousand American Earth scientists found that 90 per cent of climate scientists, and over 97 per cent of the most research-active climate researchers, accept that ".. *human activity is a significant contributing factor in changing mean global temperature*". [46] A second American survey a year later reached a similar conclusion. [47]

Climate change sceptics on the other hand may have genuine concerns about the explanations of what is causing global warming. This can be due to real misunderstandings of the science - climate science is a very complex field - or to the filter mentioned above that means they selectively favour evidence that backs up their existing beliefs while more or less ignoring evidence that goes against their beliefs. This is what psychologists call confirmation bias.

A group of Australian scientists looked into people's attitudes in considerable detail. [48] They synthesised the results of 25 polls and 171 academic studies across 56 nations concerned with people's attitudes to climate change. Surprisingly they found that people's values and ideologies, worldviews and political affiliation (the latter most of all) were more important in predicting people's climate change scepticism than age, education, gender, income, subjective knowledge or even experience of extreme weather events. Under values and ideologies they found that belief in climate change is less pronounced the more people adopt what they call hierarchical and individualistic cultural values. The authors characterise such individuals as those who value elites, which can be found in hierarchically organised societies or organisations such as the military or the police. These individuals prefer the status quo, meaning they favour stability and abhor change, and free-market values.

The Australian group also found that, counterintuitively, climate change beliefs have only a small to moderate effect on the extent to which people are willing to act in climate-friendly ways. One can't help recalling the proverb that *"the road to hell is paved with good intentions"*! Examples of climate-friendly 'public' acts are petitioning on environmental issues and contributing to environmental organizations. Private acts include recycling and individual energy reduction strategies, which are the subject of this book. Perhaps it is not surprising that the link or correlation between *"various indices of policy support and climate change beliefs get smaller the more specific and concrete the measure of policy support, and the more the measure implies personal cost on behalf of the respondent."*[48]

Another, more theoretical, take on how people's behaviour is influenced by factors other than knowledge and rational argument was proposed by Icek Ajzen, a Professor of Psychology at the University of Massachusetts, in 1991. He called it the Theory of Planned Behaviour.[49] In his theory a person's behaviour is determined by intention and we've already seen that intention does not necessarily lead to action. In turn the theory recognises that intention is influenced by three factors. These are the person's belief that the intended behaviour will produce the expected outcome, the person's perception of what is normal behaviour and the person's perception of factors they think may control their intended action.

These results and ideas, although very interesting, seem only to push the problem back one stage. They suggest that getting people to change their behaviour in ways that reduce their carbon emissions is going to be a tall order without understanding why it is that people adopt their particular values and views of the world in the first place. Is it from their experiences in life, their upbringing or even, in some strange way, their genetic make-up? The latter suggestion is one that has been studied by political scientists. [50] Finding the answers to such questions could be very influential in understanding people's attitudes to, and willingness to act on, climate change.

There is evidence on the other hand that while the general public, at least in the UK, believe the world's climate is changing they feel relatively uninformed about, or are uninterested in, the findings of climate science, and a sizable minority do not trust climate scientists to tell the truth about climate change.[51] This suggests there is a serious problem of open communication between climate scientists and the public which needs to be overcome before climate change mitigation can be successfully tackled by the whole of society in the UK. But, as is well known in this regard, facts are not enough. Nor can climate scientists be expected to successfully change people's underlying values and political allegiances.

If you find yourself in the sceptics camp or are uncertain about the science of climate change I suggest that you refer to the reading material referenced in the heading 'How the world is warming' at the beginning of this chapter. As a scientist, and not even a climate scientist at that, I am unable to suggest how, if you are sceptical, you might reconsider your political allegiance but at least the above discussion may help you to reflect on why you hold the views that you do!

What needs to be done and when

Governments meet every year under the auspices of the United Nations Framework Convention on Climate Change (UNFCCC). At the third annual meeting in Kyoto, Japan in 1997 the Kyoto Protocol was negotiated which set legally binding obligations on developed countries to reduce their greenhouse gas emissions. But progress since 1997 in deciding how to combat

20

or mitigate climate change has been slow. At the 2010 meeting in Cancún, Mexico politicians adopted a target of staying under 2°C global warming. Yet leading climate scientists now warn that even approaching 1.5°C warming will be dangerous, particularly for developing countries which are more vulnerable to rising sea level.[52]

An important UNFCCC annual meeting occurred in Paris in December 2015. It produced the Paris Agreement which, while acknowledging the dangers of global warming of even as little as 1.5°C, seems unlikely to achieve the desired result. This is largely because none of the agreement will be legally binding on the 195 countries which took part in Paris or on the 180 parties which had signed up by 3 August 2016. Meeting the aims of the agreement also depends on all countries providing detailed accounts of their carbon emissions on a regular basis. This will be especially challenging for developing countries which will need to train up a cohort of carbon accounting specialists.[53]

It is very clear that the world has been moving, and continues to move, quite fast in the direction of global warming that will affect all countries in unpleasant and costly ways. So how much time do we have? One very important piece of research which was carried out in preparing for the IPCC's Fifth Assessment reports provides an answer to this question. Scientists used computer models to see how four different greenhouse gas emissions scenarios (called Representative Concentration Pathways by the IPCC) for the rest of this century would affect the global temperature. Each scenario made different assumptions about patterns and rates of economic and population growth, demographic change, and factors such as developments in technology and policy.[54]

The important result from the IPCC was obtained after running a large number of simulations of the four different scenarios in the 21st century. The IPCC concluded that *"Multiple lines of evidence*

21

indicate a strong, consistent, almost linear relationship between cumulative CO_2 emissions and projected global temperature change to the year 2100." The phrase 'almost linear relationship' means that if we can estimate the cumulative CO_2 emissions, from historical data that are relatively easily available and we make some assumptions about future emissions too, then quite simply we can predict future global temperatures. This is a very powerful result. Conversely, if we wish to set a temperature limit to global warming we can see how large the world's cumulative emissions may be in order to stay within that limit.

There are those who like to cast doubt on the results of computer climate simulations but realistically they are the best tool we have for predicting the future because they are based on the laws of physics and chemistry. Today computer simulations are used to make predictions in many walks of life from economic predictions (which are not based on immutable laws!) to ensuring that supermarkets are stocked with sufficient turkeys for Christmas.

To illustrate the point let's take as a starting point the fact that some 1890 billion tonnes of CO_2 had already been emitted by 2011 since 1861-1880.[55] But the computer modelling suggests that to have a 66 per cent chance of not exceeding 2°C of warming since the late 19th century humanity's emissions must be less than 2900 billion tonnes CO_2.[56] Thus we see that the world had an allowance or budget of only around 2900 - 1890 = about 1000 billion tonnes to emit from 2011 and only 1000 − (4 x 35) = 860 billion tonnes from the end of 2015 (four years later) since global emissions from fossil fuels are now around 35 billion tonnes CO_2 per year.[57,58] But the situation is even worse than these figures suggest because they exclude significant emissions until the end of the century from cement production and deforestation which together are estimated to be about 210 billion tonnes in total. This leaves mankind with a scant 650 billion tonnes before we must

22

stop all emissions (or reach net zero carbon emissions as the scientists would say)[59] if 2°C warming is to be avoided with some degree of certainty. At the current global rate of emissions (35 billion tonnes of CO_2 per year) this suggests we have only 650/35 or 19 years in which to put things right.[60] This is a very short period of time in which to stop fossil fuel emissions worldwide and move to a global society which largely depends on net zero carbon sources of energy.

Exactly how can the world find a way to limit global warming to not more than 1.5°C by 2100? Work by the International Institute for Applied Systems Analysis in Austria has shown that it is already too late to avoiding breaching 1.5°C at some point but it is possible to envisage a scenario, based on several assumptions, whereby the world has warmed by 2°C in 2050 but then returns to 1.5°C by the end of the century.[61]

Today most UK (and hopefully overseas) politicians should be aware of the urgency of the situation. I know my Member of Parliament has been told so several times, yet many politicians seem to be in denial about what needs to be done. The UK government in 2016[62] could only imagine business as usual in pursuit of endless economic growth and gave little more than a nod, if that, to the urgent need to save energy and to invest in renewable sources of energy with immediate effect. The Canadian author, social activist and filmmaker Naomi Klein has described at length how many politicians appear to be in thrall to big business and large international corporations.[63]

There is hope at a more local level however. The mayors of over 1000 cities in the USA, representing almost 89 million out of 322 million citizens, and including New York, Washington DC, Los Angeles and San Francisco, have signed up to the U.S. Conference of Mayors Climate Protection Agreement.[64] The Agreement aims to *"advance the goals of the Kyoto Protocol through leadership and action"*. In Europe the Covenant of Mayors, with almost

6,800 signatories, only 30 of whom are from the UK (where most mayors have a non-executive function), has brought together mayors committed to implementing EU climate and energy objectives on their territory. In the UK several cities have established a reputation for energy saving and sustainable lifestyles. Bristol was the European Green Capital for 2015 and has made improvements in transport such as cycling, electric cars, and bus rapid transit.[65] Other cities that have established similar reputations include Newcastle-upon-Tyne, Leicester, Brighton, London, Leeds, Coventry, Plymouth, Edinburgh and Sheffield.[66]

But if only a few politicians, at national or local levels, are capable of action let's investigate what we individually, as major users of energy and consumers of products, can do by ourselves.

Summary

- It is almost completely certain that mankind is causing the relatively rapid climate change we see today and the world is getting warmer as a result.

- Worldwide, extreme weather events occur more often. They are becoming more severe and cause increasing amounts of damage in terms of infrastructure and human deaths.

- Sea level is estimated to rise by up to 1 metre by the end of this century. The IPCC has noted that many small island states are at risk of disappearing beneath the waves. Rising sea level is putting millions of people in coastal cities at risk and will eventually cause affected populations to move to higher ground.

- Climate change is predicted to be the biggest threat to global health in the 21st century.

- It is likely that some species will be unable to move fast enough to keep up with expected changes in climate or that their preferred habitats are too fragmented for them to successfully migrate to adjacent, more favourable locations. They will become extinct, at least locally.

Summary (continued)

- *Although practically all climate scientists agree that the current rapid climate change is man-made the general public does not always feel sufficiently well informed to be able to agree.*

- *People's attitude to climate change, and their willingness to act to mitigate it, are largely dependent on their political affiliation.*

- *Research suggests that the world has less than 20 years to get to net zero carbon emissions consistent with a 66 per cent chance of warming staying below 2°C.*

- *The Paris Agreement of December 2015 is an encouraging sign but the measures agreed are quite insufficient to reach the target of less than 2°C, let alone 1.5°C, global warming.*

- *It may already be too late to avoiding breaching 1.5°C warming at some point but it is possible to envisage a scenario whereby the world has warmed by 2°C in 2050 but then returns to 1.5°C by the end of the century.*

- *Encouraging steps are being taken at a local level by politicians in some countries.*

CHAPTER 2: HUMANITY'S INSATIABLE DEMAND FOR ENERGY

Although many people are comfortable with the argument that climate change today has to be tackled by humanity cutting its carbon emissions from using fossil fuels (as well as from other actions such as changes in land use) this is not true of everyone. Here I shall present other arguments from a different perspective which can also lead to marked reductions in the consumption of fossil fuels and in the growth of carbon emissions. This is that the world's insatiable demand for energy means that we shall soon need to find alternative, sustainable, more secure, non-fossil fuel sources of energy that can replace existing fossil-fuel sources as they become depleted.

The global consumption of energy has increased markedly since 1971, and at an increasing rate since around 2000, largely due to an increase in coal production by China and the rest of Asia[67] although there is now evidence that China's coal consumption peaked in 2013.[68] Perhaps partly because of the need to curb severe air pollution in its cities, China's 13th Five-Year Plan (for 2016-2020) reinforces the country's shift away from coal.[69] Global energy consumption doubled between 1973 and 2013. In 2010, 68 per cent of mankind's greenhouse gas emissions, mostly carbon dioxide, came from the generation of energy.[70] In 2013, 82 per cent of the world's primary energy supply came from fossil fuels.

The global production of crude oil from outside the USA has now plateaued.[71] This statement excludes the large production of shale oil from the USA since around 2010 (see later in this chapter). It is now getting to the point where some fossil fuels can no longer be exploited in an economic fashion. In addition, in today's turbulent world a case can be made that countries should increase their national energy security. In particular, it can be argued that the UK should source more of the energy that it requires from within its own borders rather than relying, as it does now, on significant and growing amounts of imported energy.

I hope that I can persuade those unconvinced by the purely climate change arguments of Chapter 1 that this second approach will lead not only to less dependence on fossil fuels and to the greater use of sources of renewable energy but to further reductions in our carbon emissions.

Fossil fuels are finite

My starting point is that fossil fuels, like all other natural resources on Earth, are a finite resource. Although the geological processes that created these resources, often many tens of millions of years ago, may continue today, they operate infinitely more slowly than the rate at which the resources are now being extracted and consumed. Mankind's rampant exploitation of resources is beginning to come up against the buffers in the sense that either the resources are running out or that, sometimes in addition, they are becoming too expensive to extract.

Let's take oil as an example of a finite resource. As long ago as the 1950s an American oil geologist named King Hubbert, who worked for the Shell oil company, started to think about the finite lives of US oil and coal fields. He noted that *"we can assume with complete assurance that the industrial exploitation of the fossil fuels will consist in the progressive exhaustion of an initially fixed supply to which there will be no significant addition during the period of our interest"*.[72] He plotted oil and coal production against time for different regions and found that at first they all followed a similarly shaped curve of exponentially increasing production. Of course this is unsustainable because the resource is finite and he showed that such curves eventually reach a maximum, in other words they peak, and then decline following a roughly symmetric, bell-shaped curve.

Hubbert's discovery led to the concept of peak oil. If we jump forward 50 years we find that global peak oil was supposedly reached in 2006.[73] This date is one of any number of estimates available today but the essential truth is that a peak in the production of conventional oil, if not passed already, is imminent within a few years.[74] This doesn't mean that conventional oil has now run out but it does signify that about half of the known reserves have already been extracted. Other factors such as global economics and politics may be at work too but the basic truth of Hubbert's discovery remains.

A complication when considering peak oil is the fact that although conventional oil production has peaked, or may be about to peak, global production of oil continues to meet demand because of the expansion of shale oil extraction in the USA. This explains why in February 2015 the Financial Times newspaper reported that the *"US shale oil boom masks declining global supply".*[75] The extraction of shale oil uses a technique, similar to that used in the extraction of shale gas, which depends on hydrofracturing or 'fracking' to encourage oil to flow from the rock. Fracking has been an important source of oil and gas in the USA where production has been vigorous since 2010. But now extraction is proving to be problematic and relatively short-lived as operators find that wells experience rapid declines in production rates and quality.[76]

Outside the USA the discovery of new oil fields is not keeping up with the rate at which oil is being extracted from the ground. In fact oil is said to be being consumed four times faster than it is being discovered.[77] Why are new oil fields not being discovered fast enough to match production? The answer is that the easier to find and easier to exploit fields, the so-called low-hanging fruit, have already been found. Now new fields are either much smaller

29

or else they lie much deeper in the Earth or, if offshore, under deeper water. All these factors make the fields less profitable. Weather is another important factor that limits accessibility to, and operations in, new fields, for example in the Arctic Ocean and around its margins. Finally, there is now strong societal pressure on oil companies to reduce their operations because of the widespread recognition that the use of their products is driving climate change. This has led to a growing movement to disinvest (divest) from fossil fuel companies.

A measure of energy imbalance

Although, as a scientist, I prefer to stay away from economic arguments (but see Chapter 10), I did just mention the declining profitability of getting oil out of the ground. A contributing factor is what economists call the Energy Return On energy Invested or EROI for short. Clearly if you have to expend more energy on extracting oil than you gain from the oil itself (EROI less than 1) then, ignoring the possibility that the energy used to extract the oil costs less than the value of the energy obtained from the oil, no sensible bank or investor will lend you money for such a foolish enterprise. But in reality an EROI of considerably more than 1 is estimated to be necessary to make the procedure economic or even profitable. As one survey reported *"The ecologist Charles Hall has extended the debate by … demonstrating that as oil dwindles, so does EROI. It began with a ratio of over 100 in the 19th Century, but is going down because it costs more and more energy to get oil out of the ground as reservoirs get deeper (under the sea or ground) and refining costs rise as oil grade declines. EROI for oil stood around 40 in the US in 2005, is below 10 for deep oil, and around 2 for shale oil."*[73] Shale oil has a low EROI partly because of the considerable amount of energy required to fracture or frack the rocks. A recent study showed that oil, as used in a small way in the UK to generate electricity, has an

30

EROI of only 1.7 where the energy return (output) is measured in kilowatt.hours (kWh).[78,79]

Energy security

To put the UK's energy security situation in context it is useful to consider what has been happening within the European Union (EU). Eurostat, the EU's statistical branch, reports that the production of primary energy in the EU's 28 member countries (EU-28) was 15.4 per cent lower in 2013 than it had been a decade earlier. Primary energy is defined as the raw energy found in nature, such as coal, oil, natural gas or hydropower, which has not been subjected to any conversion or transformation process. The decrease in EU-28 primary energy production is explained, at least in part, by supplies of raw materials becoming exhausted, as discussed above, and/or by producers considering the exploitation of limited resources to have become uneconomic, the EROI factor again.

The EU-28 rely on fuel imports to varying degrees. As a whole, Eurostat tells us, *"more than half (53.2 %) of the EU-28's gross inland energy consumption in 2013 came from imported sources."* 44 per cent of all solid fuel consumed, 88 per cent of all crude oil and 65 per cent of all natural gas were imported. There was an increasing dependence on energy imports from non-member countries such as Russia, Colombia and Norway.[80]

The UK finds itself in a very similar situation. The good news is that the UK's consumption of primary energy, adjusted for seasonally varying temperature, has declined by 17 per cent since 2005. The reason appears to be partly a reduced demand for heating (the winters have been warmer) but presumably other factors such as more efficient central heating boilers, better building insulation and more efficient road vehicles also played a part. However, the UK's use of energy from centralised electricity-generating power stations is remarkably inefficient; only about

31

one third (35.6%) of the energy supplied to a coal-burning power station is eventually utilised by consumers as electricity with the remaining two-thirds being lost as waste heat, by the power station consuming electricity and in the transmission and distribution of electricity through the national grid.[81] Nuclear (39.1%) and combined cycle gas turbine (48%) power stations perform slightly better.

In 2004 the UK became a net importer of fuel, that is imports exceeded exports, and this difference has continued on an upward trend ever since.[82] In 2015 the UK produced 62 per cent of its oil, gas, coal, electricity and bioenergy and imported the rest. Only in the case of coal did imports, principally from Russia, USA and Colombia, exceed home production.[83,84] Over 30 per cent of imported energy comes from Norway as crude oil and gas and just under 25 per cent, mostly crude oil and petroleum products, from other overseas sources which each contribute less than four per cent. Other gas suppliers are Qatar and the Netherlands. Russia provides 15 per cent of our imported energy. Import levels of oil and gas are expected to rise to 74 per cent by 2030.[85] The UK is increasingly connected to continental Europe by a network of electrical cable interconnectors. This enables surplus electricity, often from renewable sources, to be imported or exported to countries such as France, the Netherlands and Ireland and, in future, to Belgium, Norway, Denmark[86] and possibly Iceland.

Meanwhile UK North Sea production of crude oil has fallen steadily and in 2015 was around a third of what it was in 1999.[87] One industry leader has warned that the current low price of oil could destroy the UK oil industry.[88] Similarly, UK gas production has fallen steadily and in 2015 was just over a third of what it was in 2000.[89] This rather grim picture, so different from the end of the 20th century, shows that the UK is fast becoming more dependent on energy imports and therefore more exposed to the uncertain outcomes of international events. Even so, if it is some consolation, in 2013 there were 19 EU countries more dependent on energy imports than the UK.[80]

Shale gas as an alternative energy source?

How can the UK become less dependent on energy imports, some of which come from countries that might in future conceivably be less willing to sell their fossil fuels to us? Given the decline in North Sea oil and gas production and the resulting energy security issue the present government has set its sights on exploiting hydrofracturing (fracking) for shale gas in the UK. Potentially, renewable energy sourced in the UK can also contribute significantly to energy security. Some brief comments follow on why fracking is not desirable in the context of climate change and why this approach is unlikely to be successful.

First, shale gas is a fossil fuel. If global warming is to stay within the 2°C, let alone the 1.5°C, threshold then to avoid the dangerous consequences, as recognised in the COP21 Paris Agreement, fossil fuels must stay in the ground or at least be used without emitting CO_2 to the atmosphere. This conclusion is based on a ground-breaking piece of research published in 2015 when two UK scientists compiled estimates of the quantities, locations and nature of the world's oil, gas and coal reserves and resources.[90] On the basis of this information they explored the implications of the 2°C limit to warming on fossil fuel production and use in different parts of the world. In effect they calculated the emissions that will arise from burning the catalogued fossil fuel reserves. They were able to show, using the climate modelling referred to in Chapter 1, that to have at least a 50:50 chance of not exceeding the 2°C limit, *"... globally, a third of oil reserves, half of gas reserves and over 80 per cent of current coal reserves should remain unused from 2010 to 2050"*.[91] Although some of the existing fossil fuel reserves will need to be used to enable a smooth transition to a non-fossil fuel world it is now clearly foolhardy to search for and extract yet more fossil fuels such as shale gas. Such activities should end now; period. In general from now on further fossil fuel exploration should not even be considered.[92]

But there are other reasons to abhor shale gas. Shale gas is essentially the same as natural gas which consists largely of the powerful greenhouse gas methane. It is an incontrovertible fact that methane in the atmosphere has the potential to contribute to global warming 28 times more effectively than carbon dioxide over a period of 100 years (and to be 84 times worse over 20 years).[93] Potentially this means that fracking may release a highly climate-damaging gas (in addition to releasing carbon dioxide when the gas is subsequently burnt). The fracking operation is open not only to unplanned methane escapes both during the flow of gas from the well after fracking has taken place and during onsite gas processing and storage before onward delivery but also from the transmission pipelines.

In the USA, which has the most developed fracking industry, many investigators have monitored gas escapes, making measurements from the ground, from the air and using satellites, around sites where fracking has occurred or is going on. The results are quite alarming. A recent study using satellites estimates that, in two areas where fracking of oil reservoirs has been widespread, methane leakage of around ten per cent of total production has occurred.[94] Data from the same study over the Marcellus shale area, which has been widely fracked for natural gas, were not adequate to provide a quantitative estimate of leakage but two other studies estimate a gas leakage rate of 2.8-17.3 per cent of total production from the same area[95] and 6.2-11.7 per cent from an area in Utah.[96] However it was shown in a separate study in 2012 that [I emboldened some of the text] *"... new natural gas power plants produce net climate benefits relative to efficient, new coal plants using low gassy coal on all time frames* **as long as leakage in the natural gas system is less than 3.2% from well through delivery at a power plant.**"[97] In other words, given the suggested leakage rates of around ten per cent, supplying fracked gas to power stations may be even worse for the climate than burning coal, that is relatively gas-free, instead!

Predictably UK politicians will say that the UK has the best regulations in the world and, on paper, this might conceivably be correct. But where, in times of austerity, will the trained staff who are sufficiently skilled and experienced to carry out regular and unannounced inspections of fracking sites, and possibly the financial resources to support them (if not covered by the licence fee), be found?

The final nails in the coffin of fracking for gas in the UK are likely to be the much less geologically favourable and smaller sedimentary basins in this country (the shaly rocks containing gas are found in thick sedimentary deposits which geologists call basins). Even the several prospective gas areas identified within the relatively large 150 mile by 80 mile Bowland-Hodder Shale of central Britain are minute compared to the size of US basins. For example, the length of the very productive US Marcellus basin from northeast to southwest is greater than that of England from north to south! Further, the British Geological Survey (BGS) has already suggested that *"No significant shale gas resource is recognised in the Jurassic of the Weald Basin."*[98]; this basin extends from Wiltshire to Kent in southern England. In addition the economics of fracking in the USA are currently poor with concerns that oversupply has caused gas prices to tumble and raised fears that loans to operating companies will not be repaid. Lastly, in England[99] there have been vigorous objections to fracking by local communities in the potentially affected areas largely on the grounds of risks to health (pollution of drinking water) and damage to the environment especially in protected areas.[100] These objections are unlikely to go away.

35

Can coal be a sustainable energy source?

Coal is one fossil fuel that still exists in abundance in many countries and can be mined relatively easily. Indeed coal has steadily increased its contribution to total global greenhouse gas emissions since 1999. As the International Energy Agency (IEA) reported in 2015 *".. coal fills much of the growing energy demand of those developing countries (such as China and India) where energy-intensive industrial production is growing rapidly and large coal reserves exist with limited reserves of other energy sources."* Japan is also a major coal importing country. On the other hand, the Institute for Energy Economics and Financial Analysis, based in the USA, whose mission is *"to accelerate the transition to a diverse, sustainable and profitable energy economy and to reduce dependence on coal and other non-renewable energy resources."* has noted that global coal consumption, for power and heat generation, is expected to fall by two to four per cent in 2015 relative to the previous year. The fall is expected in part as consumption by China declines, as power plants are retired elsewhere and as the contribution from renewable energy increases.[101]

The IEA also reports that *"Globally, coal combustion generates the largest share of CO_2 emissions, although oil remains* [just] *the largest energy source."*[102] Coal also provides about 40% of the energy for global power generation and is likely to continue to play an important role for many years.[103] The reason for coal's large contribution to CO_2 emissions is simply that it is the dirtiest of all fossil fuels (possibly with the exception of shale gas as explained earlier). A review of the climate change arguments for and against substituting shale gas for coal in power generation have been set out by the IEA Clean Coal Centre. Not surprisingly the review notes the uncertainty, already mentioned, around how much methane actually leaks into the atmosphere during shale gas production and distribution which is fundamental to deciding whether to replace coal by gas.[104]

Nevertheless strenuous efforts have been, and are being, made to make coal a less polluting form of energy. Studies have been made of how coal can be burnt more efficiently, to produce the steam that runs the turbines that generate electricity, with the goal of advancing from 45 per cent for today's state-of-the-art power stations (UK coal-burning power stations operate at around 35.6 per cent[105]) to 50 per cent thermal efficiency.[103] Newer technologies are said to potentially reach over 60 per cent efficiency with near zero emissions of greenhouse gases. These include fuel cells integrated with coal gasification systems, chemical looping combustion in which an oxygen-containing solid material supplies oxygen to the coal or syngas fuel, and solar-coal hybrid power plants that integrate solar energy with coal-fired power systems.

Coal might be relatively 'cheap' but it is entirely unsuitable as a fuel for the 21st century. Of course, calling coal cheap neglects to count the hidden cost of damaging the global climate when the coal is burnt. A recent study showed that coal, as used in the UK to generate electricity, has a relatively low EROI of 3.6 where the energy return (output) is measured in kWh.[78]

Fossil fuels' last chance saloon

Earlier, when discussing shale gas, I wrote *"fossil fuels must stay in the ground or **at least be used without emitting CO_2 to the atmosphere**"*. The words in bold cover the sole situation where fossil fuels might be used in future without causing damage to the climate. It mainly refers to a technique called Carbon Capture and Storage or CCS for short. In the UK, or anywhere else, it is technically impractical to capture CO_2 from the emissions of tens of millions of moving petrol or diesel road vehicles or from the flues of a similar number of domestic gas and oil boilers; there are too many of them. CCS is best suited for use in power stations and large industrial plants. In principle CCS works by capturing carbon dioxide from flue gases, compressing it into a liquid and then pumping it underground into a geological formation where it can remain trapped for hundreds of years or more. In 2014 the CO_2 emissions from fossil-fuel burning power stations around the world was around 13.6 billion tonnes.[106] The IPCC Working Group III reports that in 2010 electricity production was responsible for 34 per cent of global CO_2 emissions[107] so a lot is at stake if CCS can be shown to work.

Power stations burn a variety of fuels, mainly coal and gas, at different temperatures so the technical details of how the CO_2 can be separated from the flue gases are quite complex. The processes are well described at length in a book by Peter Cook, a former Director of the British Geological Survey (BGS).[108] As he points out, the processes involved require the use of extra energy which itself is a serious constraint on the practicality of this aspect of CCS. Not surprisingly this is a topic of ongoing research. Although there is a strong case for all new power stations being fitted with CCS there are examples from around the world where CCS has been successfully retrofitted to existing power stations as well.

Given that CO_2 can be extracted from flue gases the problem arises of how to transport it to where it is going to be stored underground. In principle, although CO_2 can be transported as a gas, a liquid or a solid, the liquid form is likely to be most suitable since the technology of moving liquid CO_2 in pipelines is already widely used in the oil industry. Grids of pipelines exist within and between many countries.

Finding a site where liquid CO_2 can be stored underground is similar to exploring for oil or gas. It is important to locate a geological formation that will hold the CO_2 in place for centuries or more. It is argued that a cap rock[109] that has held natural gas in place for millions of years will safely fulfil the same function for CO_2 that is injected beneath it. One experiment was started by the Norwegian company Statoil in the Sleipner gas field of the North Sea in 1996. Statoil pumped CO_2 into a rock formation called the Utsira Sand, a deep aquifer containing salty water, and monitored the results in conjunction with the BGS by re-surveying the aquifer over several years up to 2008 using seismic exploration techniques. Spectacular time lapse seismic images (essentially vertical cross-sections) showed that the gas was retained by the cap rock and confined securely within the storage reservoir.[110,111] The Utsira Sand formation is porous. If only about 1 per cent of the volume of the sand were utilised for CO_2 storage in the empty pores between the sand grains, it is estimated that this would be sufficient to store 50 years of emissions from around 20 coal-fired, or nearly 50 gas-fired, 500 MW power-stations!

The Boundary Dam power station in Saskatchewan, Canada, which started in 2014, is possibly the first commercial scale CCS operation in the world. It is due to be operational at the end of 2016 and is expected to capture 1 billion tonnes of CO_2 each year. CCS was retrofitted to a coal-burning power station and a 66 km long pipeline was built to connect the site to an operational oil field. Most of the CO_2 will be pumped underground to help extract oil from the field (a technique known as enhanced oil recovery) and the rest will be pumped into a deep brine aquifer, like the Utsira Sand in the North Sea. The Global CCS Institute recently reported that worldwide 15 large-scale CCS sites had become operational in 2015 with *"key projects in the power, iron and steel, and chemical industries to be launched in the next 18 months"*.[112] Such activity is very encouraging.

But, as an editorial comment in the journal Nature said in 2014 *"Many questions remain about the long-term viability of a serious and sustained CCS contribution to the global effort to reduce greenhouse-gas emissions, not least how to guarantee that stored carbon stays stored.*"[113] CCS has great potential to contribute to mitigating climate change but will only work, technically, geologically and economically, where the conditions are right. There is certainly a lack of political will to develop this technology in the UK. It was deeply disappointing when in November 2015 the UK government cancelled a one billion pound competition to develop CCS at the Peterhead power station, backed by Shell and the energy company SSE, and at the Drax power station.

While it is expected that eventually CCS will be used at power stations and major industrial plants research is also going on to capture CO_2 directly from the air. Such air capture technology has been under development for some years but it was recently reported that one company plans to use the captured CO_2 to create diesel fuel and another company plans to use the CO_2 to boost crop growth in greenhouses.[114]

Air pollution

A further reason to abandon fossil fuels is their effect on air pollution. One of the earliest recognitions of the damaging effects of burning coal in homes, and later in power stations, was the realisation that the resulting smoke caused smog, a combination of smoke and fog, which was the cause of many deaths from respiratory diseases. Later it was realised that sulphur emitted by coal burning led to acid rain which killed trees downwind of power stations and acidified bodies of freshwater. These 19th and 20th century problems have largely been solved by legislation and changes in technology.

However, another form of air pollution remains a global problem. The World Health Organisation (WHO), working with the University of Bath in UK, has reported that 92 per cent of the world's population, in fact almost everyone, breathes poor quality air.[115] They say that an estimated 6.5 million deaths (11.6% of all global deaths) were associated with indoor and outdoor air pollution together and exposure outdoors to air pollution has caused around 3 million deaths a year. Southeast Asia and the western Pacific are the worst affected regions. Major sources of air pollution include inefficient modes of transport, household fuel and waste burning, coal-fired power plants, and industrial activities. Many of these sources rely on the consumption of diesel derived from oil, a fossil fuel, and coal, another fossil fuel. However, some air pollution has a natural origin. For example, air quality can be influenced by dust storms, particularly in regions close to deserts.

The exhaust emissions from diesel road vehicles are the main source of air pollution today. Diesel emissions include tiny soot particles less than 2.5 millionths of a metre in size (called $PM_{2.5}$) and nitrogen dioxide which cause respiratory problems, heart attacks and strokes. Air pollution has been credited by the Royal College of Physicians with causing over 40,000 early deaths in the UK annually.[116]

Emissions from ships, which burn heavy diesel fuel, in national and international waters are another cause of concern which is gradually being tackled today by the International Maritime Organization (IMO).[117] The IMO has brought in regulations that ensure the progressive reduction globally in emissions of oxides of sulphur and nitrogen, and particulate matter. They have also introduced emission control areas (ECAs) to further reduce emissions of those air pollutants in designated sea areas. Again, the fuel that ships use is derived from oil, a fossil fuel.

Airports can also be hot spots of air pollution not only from aircraft, at ground level and relatively low altitudes, burning kerosene derived from fossil fuel but also from the large number of road vehicles used to transport people and freight to and from the site. A research study of 12 airports in California found that the poisonous gas carbon monoxide was emitted by taxiing aircraft which *"significantly impacts the health of local residents*".[118] The authors found increased respiratory and heart-related admissions to hospitals for people living within 10 km of an airport.

There are also concerns, particularly in the USA, about the escape of various gases from oil and natural gas exploration activities. The gases include hydrogen sulphide and hydrocarbons, such as methane and benzene, which is a known human carcinogen. Hydrocarbons and nitrogen oxides can also, under certain weather conditions, react to produce ozone which is harmful to breathe. Although anecdotal evidence suggests these activities may coincide with specific health problems among some local populations the evidence of a causal link has yet to be proved.[119,120]

While there are technical and legislative solutions to many air pollution problems it is costly and time-consuming to ensure that they are put into practice, especially on a global scale. Air pollution, and its health impacts on humans, provides yet more arguments to move rapidly away from fossil fuels to renewable sources of energy.

The role of nuclear power

The big advantage of a nuclear power station is that, once built, it is cheap to run and can provide baseload energy day in day out for relatively small marginal CO_2 emissions per kWh. Baseload energy is that constant background energy required to service constant demand. France has depended on nuclear power to supply 75 per cent of its electricity for some years and thereby has provided relatively cheap energy, which today costs about 16.9 €cents per kWh including various taxes.[121]

Even though a nuclear power station produces relatively small CO_2 emissions in operation it is estimated to have a significant carbon footprint over its entire life. The reason is that energy, and therefore emissions, are involved in mining, transporting and

42

processing uranium ore, in using large quantities of cement in construction, in decommissioning the plant and eventually in disposing of, or storing, the radioactive waste. Detailed life-cycle analyses of the production of energy by nuclear power stations have led to a range of estimates from 60 to 134 g CO_2 per kWh.[122] For the UK's reactors it has been estimated that emissions are at least 32 g CO_2 per kWh without including emissions from waste disposal.[123] Although less than emissions from fossil fuel power stations these emissions are not as low as most sources of renewable energy.

In 2013 the UK relied on 15 nuclear reactors to supply 19 per cent of its grid electricity. Fourteen are advanced gas-cooled reactors (AGR) built between the late 1970s and 1980s and one is a newer pressurised water reactor (PWR). All but one of the AGR reactors are due for retirement within the next decade. However in February 2016 EDF, the owner of eight of these reactors, announced that the Heysham 1 and Hartlepool reactors will have their lives extended by five years until 2024, while the Heysham 2 and Torness reactors will see their closure dates pushed back by seven years to 2030.[124]

Lack of UK capital investment and research in new nuclear reactors since the 1980s has led to the current situation in which there are rising concerns about a growing gap between electricity supply and demand.[125,126] Nuclear power plants of the PWR type, called the European Pressurised Reactor (EPR), are planned to be built in the UK at Hinkley Point C and at Sizewell C. Construction of the Hinkley Point C power station has yet to start. An EPR has been under construction at Flamanville, France since December 2007 but it has encountered technical difficulties and budget overruns and the reactor is not expected to start up until the end of 2018.[127] A similar situation exists at the Olkiluoto site in Finland, the only other European site where an EPR reactor is being built, where construction of the first reactor was started in 2005 but because of technical difficulties start-up is currently not expected to happen until 2018 as well.[128]

Besides the considerable delays in construction, the huge budgets required and cost overruns, nuclear power also suffers from two other major disadvantages which are, a) the cost of decommissioning - the Nuclear Decommissioning Agency received over £2 billion from the UK government in 2015/2016 - and b) the lack of acceptable sites, so far, at which to store the high-level radioactive waste which remains dangerous to life for thousands of years.

A different technology, already being used elsewhere, is described as small modular reactors (SMRs) which are defined as those generating up to 300 million watts of electricity[129], enough to supply around 400,000 homes. The UK has yet to make a decision on installing such reactors.

Lastly it should be noted that nuclear fuel is made from enriched uranium ores which, like fossil fuels, are a finite resource. They too are subject to limited supply as high-grade ores run out. The current EROI of nuclear power in the UK has been estimated to be as high as 30.[78] Nevertheless it is evident that, **at least over the next decade or so in which mankind has to take firm action to mitigate climate change**, nuclear power in the UK is unlikely to be able to provide additional reliable sources of electricity.

Can renewable energy be the solution?

If you have read this far you will realise that fossil fuels are rapidly coming to the end of the road as a viable source of fuels for electricity and heat generation unless there is widespread development of carbon capture and storage within a few decades and possibly some technology to directly extract CO_2 from the air. Further, as already explained, nuclear power cannot provide a long-term solution because the uranium fuel is a finite resource and there are severe practical problems around handling the long-lasting, high-level radioactive waste. At least in the UK and continental Europe, nuclear power seems unable to rise to the immediate challenge of providing a reliable source of electricity over the next decade or so. Yet firm steps have to be taken, not only to meet electricity demand in the UK as coal-burning power stations are closed down, but also globally to reduce emissions to mitigate climate change if the 2°C warming threshold is not to be breached. The National Grid, in all its future energy scenarios, forecasts a growing percentage of electric cars up to 2040 and modest changes, both up and down, to annual electricity demand relative to 2015.[130]

And so this brings us to renewable energy which, other than a declining use of fossil fuels during a transitional period of a few decades to net zero carbon emissions, appears to be the only way in which the UK can generate the electricity required to support the kind of society that we live in today.

Renewable energy has been used by mankind for centuries in the form of wind, running water and tides and even by burning wood for heating and cooking. The great advantage of renewable energy is that it uses essentially infinite sources of energy. This energy comes directly (as solar radiation) or indirectly (as wind, rain and snow, and biofuels as well as waves and ocean currents) from the Sun or from the orbit of the Moon around the Earth, which drives the tides. There is also geothermal energy which has been harvested in areas of volcanic activity such as Iceland and New Zealand.

With modern technology, once the initial capital outlay has been made, the running costs and operational CO_2 emissions of renewable energy are minimal. This is in stark contrast to fossil fuels which, except for the current low prices driven by distorted oil and gas markets, are set to rise in price as fuels become less accessible, less economic and eventually start to run out. But it has to be recognised that renewables consume finite resources in their initial construction. For example, the permanent magnets in wind turbine generators contain rare earth elements which are sourced predominantly from China.[131] In principle such resources should be recyclable.

Renewable energy is also superior to fossil fuel energy on other grounds. One recent review of renewable energy has concluded *"Our analysis indicates that the large-scale implementation of wind, PV* [photovoltaics], *and CSP* [concentrating solar power] *has the potential to reduce pollution-related environmental impacts of electricity production".* The review refers principally to coal-burning power stations, with or without carbon capture and storage. The impacts are the emission of greenhouse gases, which drive climate change, the pollution of rivers and lakes by chemicals that are detrimental to their ecosystems (ecotoxicity), the depletion of oxygen in freshwater bodies (eutrophication), and exposure to PM_{10} particulate-matter.[132]

Renewable energy is being implemented worldwide at a growing rate. In 2014 renewable sources of energy contributed 9.3 per cent of the world's energy needs.[133] In Europe the impact was even more dramatic. In 2014 renewable energy provided 27.5 per cent of the electricity consumed within the EU-28.[134] The UK lags somewhat behind the EU as a whole because in 2015 just 24.6 per cent of UK electricity came from renewable sources.[135]

Nevertheless there remains a school of thought that renewables alone will not meet the demand and that the UK will have to rely, at least to some extent, on nuclear energy and/or 'clean coal'. Quantitative objections to relying entirely on renewable energy were summarised by the late David Mackay, Chief Scientific Advisor at DECC from 2009-2014, in his book *Sustainable energy – without the hot air.* He argued that to generate electricity from onshore wind and biofuels an area

46

equivalent to around 45 per cent of the land in England and Wales would have to be given over to wind farms or growing biofuels (mainly the latter).[136] And this estimate did not include land taken up already by buildings and infrastructure, such as roads, railways and airports, and land needed to grow food. In May 2016 he called the idea of relying entirely on renewable energy an *"appalling delusion".*[136] Unfortunately such arguments take insufficient account of the speed with which greenhouse gas emissions must be cut today to mitigate global warming and the problems facing EPR reactors and the lack of proven CCS technology in the UK, as already mentioned. Nor do such arguments allow for the positive benefits of cutting energy demand, and therefore emissions, from the adoption of suitable technologies, such as building low (or zero) carbon homes and the widespread adoption of more efficient and fewer road vehicles, or the potential effects of changes in people's behaviour. These issues are addressed in later chapters.

Getting to net zero carbon

'Net zero carbon' means a situation where carbon emissions, if any, are balanced or exceeded by the natural and man-made take up of CO_2 from the atmosphere. Clearly the use of renewable energy can play a large part in achieving net zero carbon.

Numerous published quantitative scenarios suggest how globally and nationally individual countries can achieve zero carbon by 2050. A list of five global or regional scenarios and 18 national scenarios, selected from over 100 such plans, has been published by the Centre for Alternative Technology (CAT), based in Machynlleth in Wales, working with Track0, a London-based not-for-profit organisation.[137] 'Road maps' showing how 100 per cent renewable energy can be reached by 139 countries have also been released by researchers at Stanford University in California.[138] These studies really do show that, given the will and a sense of urgency by governments, reaching net zero carbon is feasible by 2050.

In the UK, how can electricity generation and heating systems be reorganised so as to depend on growing contributions from renewable energy which may eventually come close to 100 per cent? Several groups, notably CAT in its series of *Zero Carbon Britain* reports, have already demonstrated quantitatively that, with a mix of different renewables, as well as big savings in energy consumption and improvements in energy efficiency, this is possible.[139] The call in the latest CAT report for 'zero heroes' emphasises that there is a steep hill to climb to make it happen. It is worth summarising the report's conclusions here:

- *"Climate* [mitigation] *action is pro-human development and pro-fairness*
- *Time is up for wasteful energy use*
- *Time is up for fossil fuels - the technologies to achieve zero emissions by mid-century already exist*
- *If we manage the transition well, we can reach zero emissions without disruption to industry or consumers*
- *Integrated net zero scenarios* [must] *cover energy, transport, built environment, industry, agriculture and land use*
- *Multiple co-benefits include stronger and more stable economics, increased access to energy without air pollution and productive and biodiverse forests and land use*
- *Everyone must be ambitious - we must all pull together."*

Even so, many serious practical problems have to be overcome in detail such as dealing with the intermittency of wind and solar, the smart use of energy, so that demand always matches supply, the storage of electricity for when supply exceeds demand or when demand exceeds supply, and the use of biomass as a source of energy alongside CCS to dispose of the resulting CO_2.

It is not my intention to get into a detailed discussion here of how the UK could transition from today's system of mainly centralised, inefficient, fossil-fuel power stations to one with more dispersed sources of energy from a variety of mainly renewable sources (see reports mentioned above). I wish only to point out that this is the direction in which the UK should move rapidly and that better-off individual homeowners can play their part by, among other things, improving home insulation, reducing their energy demand and changing their transport behaviour, and by installing renewable energy in their homes where appropriate. This will not only help the UK to cut its emissions but also indirectly protect the environment and be a way to invest in viable and mature green technologies for the future.

Summary

- *Fossil fuels are a finite resource. They are becoming harder to extract and, eventually, will be in shorter supply and more expensive.*

- *Conventional oil is at, or approaching, peak production rates.*

- *The UK is becoming increasingly dependent on imported energy as North Sea production of oil and gas declines. This has security implications.*

- *It is time to stop extracting and burning fossil fuels most of which, to avoid 2°C, let alone 1.5°C, warming, should stay in the ground.*

- *Because, in the USA, roughly ten per cent of shale gas is lost during its production and onward transmission shale gas is potentially even more climate damaging than coal and therefore cannot be a solution to the UK's energy needs.*

- *Coal makes a large contribution to CO_2 emissions because it is the dirtiest of all fossil fuels (possibly with the exception of shale gas).*

Summary (continued)

- *The capture and storage underground of CO_2 emitted by fossil-fuel burning power stations offers one way to mitigate climate change but the technology remains immature mainly from a lack of investment.*

- *Nuclear power is at a low ebb and is unlikely to be able to respond to the UK's energy needs in the near future. Existing plant is approaching the end of its life. Over the period of time in which mankind has to take firm action to mitigate climate change, new nuclear power in the UK is unlikely to be able to provide a reliable source of electricity.*

- *Given the problems with fossil fuels, carbon capture and storage, and nuclear power, renewable energy appears to be today's answer to the UK's energy problems. This is an approach to which, in the right circumstances, better-off individual homeowners can contribute.*

- *Numerous quantitative studies suggest scenarios whereby the UK and other countries can achieve net zero carbon by 2050.*

CHAPTER 3: HUMANITY'S CARBON EMISSIONS

Carbon emissions by individuals on a global scale

Man-made, or anthropogenic, carbon emissions are not equally distributed among all countries, let alone among individuals in any one country. This is hardly surprising since not all countries are at the same stage of economic development and emissions are strongly correlated with the standard of living within a country. For example, the growth of the so-called middle class in China and their demand for cars, televisions and the like has been part of the reason for the rapid growth in global emissions so far in the 21st century. In 2012 China contributed 27 per cent of all global emissions.[140]

To begin to understand how we got to where the world is today, in terms of greenhouse gas emissions, it is interesting to take a look briefly at how these emissions have grown since the beginning of the industrial revolution around the middle of the 18th century. Then emissions were about three thousandths of what they are today and by the 1850s, when emissions began to climb, they had increased 'only' 20 fold.[140] The UK was one of the first countries to industrialise and this happened on the back of plentiful supplies of coal. But of course when coal is burnt it releases CO_2, among other gases, into the atmosphere. Not only were homes, steam engines in factories and steam locomotives on the railways, and later power stations, burning huge quantities of coal but a vast fleet of coal-burning ships carried goods and passengers to and from far flung parts of the British Empire. Emissions from burning coal only started to decline in the UK around 1956.[140]

Therefore it should be no surprise that although the UK contributed as little as 1.3 per cent of all global emissions in 2012 its cumulative emissions since 1750 are 5.4 per cent of all emissions since then. Even worse, as US climate scientist James Hansen claims, *"If you look at per capita contributions to cumulative emissions, the United Kingdom, the United States and Germany* [with Australia, Canada and Russia not far behind] *are by far the most responsible. China is an order of magnitude smaller, India is so small it's almost off the chart."*[141] The UK tops this list of countries with around 1210 tonnes of CO_2 emitted since 1750 for each person living in the UK today.[142]

But to return to global emissions today. At the time of the COP21 meeting convened by the UN in Paris in December 2015 the charity Oxfam, which describes itself as a global movement of people who believe that, in a world rich in resources, poverty is not inevitable, put out a media briefing. Oxfam stated that consumption by individuals, including direct and indirect energy,[143] is responsible for as much as 64 per cent of all global emissions.[144] The rest of the emissions are attributed to consumption by governments, investment (as in infrastructure) and international transport (aviation and shipping). Given the complexity and uncertainty of estimating global emissions Oxfam warn, in a technical annex, that *" all figures should be regarded as indicative of orders of magnitude, rather than exact reflections of reality."* although there is no reason to believe that the broad conclusions of the briefing are wrong. Here I consider just emissions by individuals.

It is well known, and not surprising, that on an individual level emissions are a function of people's income. Poorer people cause fewer emissions than richer people.[145] Thus Oxfam estimated that the richest ten per cent of people in the world by income, through their personal consumption of goods and services, are responsible for almost half of global emissions by individuals, whereas the poorest half of the global population is responsible for only around ten per cent of such global emissions. Oxfam states, the richest ten per cent *".... have average carbon footprints 11 times as high as the poorest half of the population, and 60 times as high as the poorest 10%. The average footprint of the richest 1% of people globally could be 175 times that of the poorest 10%."*[144] The top ten per cent of emitters live on all continents, with as many as one third of them from emerging countries.[146] Not only is this situation grossly unfair but research shows that the poorest in the world are the most vulnerable to the negative impacts of climate change. Such impacts include flooding from rising sea level and heavy rainfall, droughts (and resulting crop failures) and heat waves.

Within countries too there are inequalities. Again the Oxfam report says *"... such inequalities are horizontal as well as vertical – with women facing greater risks than men, rural communities often more exposed than urban ones and groups marginalized because of race, ethnicity or other factors likely to be disproportionately affected."* For example, in China, the country with the largest population on the planet, the richest 10.6 per cent, who live in urban areas, cause 30 per cent of the emissions yet the 47 per cent of rural Chinese are responsible for only 25 per cent of emissions.[147]

When the World Bank analysed data from 92 countries, representing well over half the global population, it found that most people live in countries where poor people (defined as the poorest 20 per cent of the national population) are more exposed to such disasters.[148] Such inequalities are not restricted to poorer or less developed countries; they can be seen even in the richest countries such as the USA[149] and Saudi Arabia.[150]

Nevertheless, inequality in emissions has decreased between countries, since the Kyoto Protocol was signed in 1998 (see Chapter 1), as a result of growing emissions from rapidly developing, poorer countries described as the China effect (which includes other so-called BRICS countries too[151]). On the other hand, at the same time, the disparity in emissions within countries has increased. By 2015 two opposing linear trends in a graph of a quantitative measure of the decreasing between-countries and increasing within-countries emissions used by Chancel and Piketty, two economists from the Paris School of Economics, had crossed over.[152] In other words the measures had become essentially the same although they do depend on an assumption that these authors had to make about how emissions can be estimated from income.[146] This graph implies that, if the two trends continue, very soon there will be greater inequality of emissions within countries, i.e. mostly between the rich and the poor, than between countries.

So what's to be done? Global emissions come from a wide range of sources, only some of which are influenced or controlled by the behaviour of individuals. For example, energy production and transport infrastructure are generally determined by governments. But if emissions are to be reduced globally I argue that one of the most important things to do is to reduce the emissions caused by the high consumption of the richest people in whatever country they live. This may achieve a reduction faster than if one depends on short-sighted, weak-willed, bureaucratic or slow-to-respond governments to make changes to infrastructure and legislation. If successful, such a strategy would have the greatest impact by persuading better-off individuals to change their lifestyle and consumption. The poorest members of the global population not unreasonably aspire to higher standards of living, such as better diets, health and housing, which in developed countries are often taken for granted.

Given the large differences previously mentioned in carbon footprints between the richest and the poorest of the global population it is not hard to imagine how if the richest people, wherever they live, gave up part of their high consumption and high emitting lifestyle they could have a large impact on global emissions. Who are these rich people and where do they live? The Oxfam report says *"The vast majority of the world's richest 10% high emitters still live in rich OECD countries, although that is slowly changing."* The 34 OECD countries are mainly in North America and the EU but also include Australia, Israel, Japan, Korea, Mexico and New Zealand. Other high emitting countries or regions, not necessarily with a large number of high emitting individuals, are Russia, South Africa, China, Latin America, the Middle East and North Africa.[146]

Let's consider some examples. Taking figures from the Oxfam briefing, the richest ten per cent of the world population (here called decile 1; a population can be divided into ten deciles (tenths) of equal size arranged or ranked in the order of some statistical measure, in this case income spent on consumption) are said to be responsible for 49 per cent of all emissions by individuals. **If the richest ten per cent of individuals were to change their lifestyles so as to reduce their emissions by half, as my own household was able to do, that would save an astonishing 24.5 per cent of global emissions by individuals (or 16 per cent of all emissions).**[153] If the number of individuals who reduce their emissions is expanded and we assume that the top ten per cent of emitters cut by half, the next ten per cent cut by 30 per cent and the next ten per cent by 20 per cent almost a third of global emissions by individuals would be saved (or 21 per cent of all emissions; see table).

These are simple and approximate sums but they emphasise that worldwide changes by individuals, and particularly by better-off individuals, can have a very significant impact on reducing global emissions and therefore on mitigating climate change. If carried out, this would be a huge step on the road to achieving near-zero-carbon emissions globally by 2050 or preferably much sooner.

The effect on global emissions of reductions made by different income deciles[144]

Income decile	Global emissions generated by individuals by decile	Assumed emissions reduction by decile	Savings referred to all emissions by individuals by decile	Savings referred to total global emissions by decile
1	49%	50%	24.5%	16.0%
2	19%	30%	5.7%	3.6%
3	11%	20%	2.2%	1.4%
Total	79%		32.4%	21.0%

I shall show in later chapters how it is possible in practice for individuals and households to make significant reductions in emissions by changes in behaviour and lifestyle. But first let's look in more detail at the distribution of emissions within one country, the UK.

The distribution of carbon emissions between UK households

In this section I look at how carbon emissions are distributed among households in Great Britain.[154] The results I shall present are based on data collected before a general election in May 2015 in which a majority Conservative government was returned to power. Between May 2015 and late 2016 this government made a variety of changes almost entirely to the detriment of attempts to save energy, increase renewable energy generation or reduce carbon emissions. Specifically, it was reported in April 2016 that government-backed energy efficiency measures installed in homes had dropped by 80 per cent since 2012.[155] At the time of writing the government's future intentions in this area appear to be largely unfavourable to reducing the UK's emissions. This approach is particularly puzzling and concerning since the UK's Climate Change Act (2008) created a target that is legally binding on governments to reduce the UK's emissions of greenhouse gases to at least 80 per cent below 1990 levels by 2050.

I wrote to my Member of Parliament asking him to find out what the government's policy on climate change was, since the only statement in the public domain at the time appeared to be a speech in November 2015 on energy policy by Amber Rudd, the then Secretary of State for Energy and Climate Change.[156] This speech emphasised getting energy from 'new gas' (shale gas), nuclear and offshore wind. I received a reply from a junior minister.[157] In his letter, while correctly stressing *"there are huge risks if we do not reduce our emissions"* he continued *"... it is important that we are pragmatic and cut carbon emissions as cost-effectively as possible. We have to demonstrate that the low carbon transition can be cost-effective and will deliver growth for the economy and affordable energy prices for consumers."* There is no recognition in this letter of either the cost of **not** mitigating climate change or of the fact that this is a matter of urgency. It has to be said that many informed observers might not consider that the evidence favours the approach outlined in Amber Rudd's speech or in the minister's reply. In any event it is not yet clear that the actions of the current government will have any immediate effect on carbon emissions by households in the UK.

The Joseph Rowntree Foundation (JRF) is an independent organisation working to inspire social change through research, policy and practice, which aims for a UK without poverty. It commissioned a report published in 2015 by the Centre for Sustainable Energy to ensure that people facing poverty are not disproportionately affected by climate change.[158] The report explored the distribution of household emissions from the consumption of energy in the home and from personal travel by private vehicle, public transport and domestic and international flights for non-business purposes. It was unusually thorough in including all travel as well as the consumption of electricity, gas and other fuels in the home. Statistics were obtained from three independently run nationally representative surveys.[159]

Although the JRF report was based on possibly the most thorough research conducted in the UK in recent times we have to realise that it considered only those sources of emissions that are most easily measured; these are often called direct emissions. Indirect emissions which result from the production or manufacture of goods that households buy, such as food, clothing and appliances, were not included and yet it is often considered that indirect emissions are comparable in amount to direct emissions.[160] Generally it is very difficult to estimate the indirect emissions associated with such goods, although more and more manufacturers are attempting to do so for their individual products. A valiant attempt to estimate the embodied emissions associated with dozens of products or actions, from sending a text message to buying a new car, can be found in the book *How bad are bananas?* by Mike Berners-Lee which is worth a read if you want to get a feel for the emissions linked to many different household goods or activities.[161] On the other hand, it is probably safe to assume that an individual or household that takes great care to minimise their direct emissions is also likely to be aware of and to minimise, at least to some extent, the indirect emissions associated with goods that they buy.

The JRF report also demonstrates the extent to which households' annual CO_2 emissions in Great Britain are influenced by a range of factors. As we might expect it shows that emissions are strongly correlated with income and that in general households with lower incomes tend to have lower than average

CO_2 emissions. The household emissions data were analysed according to 17 socio-demographic variables. The highest correlation of total emissions was with the number of cars in the household, the disposable income, the make-up of the household (such as whether or not the occupants were pensioners and the numbers of adults and children present), and the number of bedrooms (as a measure of the physical size of the home).

The most striking result was that the average annual CO_2 emissions from all sources correlated most strongly with a household's disposable income, which is the income left after paying income tax, in a linear fashion. The exception was the ten per cent of households with the greatest income. These households emitted more than expected, largely from a disproportionately greater use of international air travel. The richest ten per cent of households generate 16 per cent of total household emissions whereas the poorest ten per cent generate 5.1 per cent which is just over three times less. Therefore the inequality of household emissions within Great Britain is very much less than the estimated global inequality of individuals' emissions between the richest and poorest ten per cents which amounted to a factor of 49 as we saw in the previous section.[162] Even for international air travel, which is the source of emissions that exhibits the largest difference between rich and poor in the JRF report, the inequality factor in Great Britain is only just over ten (for emissions from household fuels, which include electricity, gas and non-metered fuels, it is 2.1, for car use 7.4, and for public transport 1.5). Despite emissions increasing from low- to high-income households in Great Britain, there remain significant variations in emissions within the ten per cent income bands across the spread of incomes, so that the highest emitting poor households have comparable emissions to the mean emissions of wealthy households.

Is the JRF report backed up by other data? An earlier survey of personal travel conducted in Oxfordshire, a county in central England, in 2004/2005 came up with an interesting observation. It found that little more than a handful of individuals in each of four typical areas (urban and rural) greatly biased the total greenhouse emissions in that area.[163] The authors express this as "... *a few are responsible for a disproportionately large share of the total*" and their results imply this was essentially down to emissions from air travel. They continued "*Overall, it is a minority of users, travelling comparatively long distances, who account for the differences between high and low quintiles.*" [a population arranged or ranked in the order of some statistical measure, in this case distance travelled, can be divided into five quintiles of equal size]. Looking at emissions from all modes of travel they conclude that 61 per cent of travel emissions came from the top 20 per cent of individuals and less than 1 per cent from the bottom 20 per cent giving an inequality factor of 90! This is more similar to the worldwide factor for individual emissions than to the same factor for Great Britain. It suggests that emissions from air travel may be a key factor in determining the carbon footprint of households (or individuals) in the UK. The authors found that the richest ten per cent of households produce the equivalent of 19.1 tonnes CO_2 each year from flying alone (equivalent to an average car being driven 66,000 miles).[164] They suggest that any eventual government intervention to reduce emissions must be targeted at this high-emitting sector of the population to be effective and conclude "*policy needs to target the gross polluters, i.e. certain subgroups of the population who are responsible for a disproportionally large share of total emissions.*"

Even so, it appears that it is not possible, when emissions from all sources are considered, to attribute a large proportion of household emissions in Great Britain to a relatively small number of households as was possible with the global statistics on individuals. Nevertheless, returning to the JRF report, it is worth making some comparable calculations. If we assume that the richest ten per cent of households (decile 1) cut their emissions from all sources by half then an 8.2 per cent saving will be made in total household emissions. If we next assume that the second and third richest ten per cents of households (deciles 2 and 3) cut their emissions by 30 per cent and 20 per cent, respectively, we find that a saving of 15 per cent of all household emissions can be made, almost twice as much as cutting from the top ten per cent alone. Finally, if on top of the second set of savings all other ten per cent income groups, except the poorest, i.e. deciles 4 to 9, make a ten per cent saving then overall a saving of just over 20 per cent can be made in total household emissions.

Earlier we saw that the Oxfam briefing stated that globally individuals account for 64 per cent of all emissions.[165] In the UK, one estimate is that household emissions from all sources, including energy, transport (including flying) and indirect emissions, accounts for a very similar figure of around 61 per cent of all emissions.[166,167] These emissions were calculated from household expenditure data and the method necessarily involved some assumptions. So, if we assume that UK households account for 61 per cent of all the UK's emissions then we can conclude that the top three deciles considered in the previous paragraph would correspond to 5.0 per cent, 2.2 per cent and 1.6 per cent, respectively, of all the UK's emissions (see table). The 20 per cent savings in household emissions made by including the additional households in deciles 4 to 9, with mean disposable annual incomes of £8,900 to £28,900 leads to a 12.2 per cent saving, or about one eighth, in total UK emissions.

In summary, if the richest ten per cent of households were to reduce their direct and indirect emissions by half, the next two richest deciles reduce emissions by 30 and 20 per cent, respectively, and the rest, bar the poorest, each reduce

emissions by 10 per cent that would save 20.2 per cent of the UK's emissions by households (or 12.2 per cent of all the UK's emissions). Although necessarily approximate, these numbers illustrate the potential contribution that households and individuals can make to reduce the UK's greenhouse gas emissions. Similar figures were arrived at in 2009 in a study of homes in the USA. These authors found that households could save 20 per cent of their direct emissions and 7.4 per cent of national emissions *'with little or no reduction in household well-being'.* [168]

In my experience making savings in emissions is not too challenging given sufficient commitment and encouragement. If around 12 per cent of the UK's total emissions can be cut by individual actions alone this is a target worth aiming for. I shall describe how such savings could be made later in the book.

The effect on UK emissions of savings made by different household income deciles. [158]

Income decile	Mean disp. inc.	Emissions by house	Assumed emm. red.	Savings rel. households	Savings rel. UK
1	74,000	16.4	50	8.2	5.0
2	44,000	14.0	30	4.2	2.2
3	35,000	13.1	20	2.6	1.6
4-9	8,900-28,900	51.9	10	5.0	3.4
Total		95		20	12

Col.2 Mean disposable annual income (GBP)
Col.3 Emissions generated by households by decile (%)
Col.4 Assumed emissions reduction by decile (%)
Col.5 Savings relative to all emissions by households (%)
Col.6 Savings relative to total UK emissions (%)

Finally it is worth seeing where, on average, within households in Great Britain, the largest sources of emissions lie. The sources in decreasing size of contribution are household fuels, private cars, international flights, public transport and domestic flights.[169] The figure for household fuels includes electricity, gas and other fuels. We can subdivide this latter emissions figure using relative proportions derived from data published by the UK government for domestic fuel consumption in 2013 into gas, electricity and other fuels (solid fuel and oil).[170] We end up with the estimates shown in the table of the average split of household emissions between different sources.

Average split of emissions in UK households

Source of emissions	Percentage of total emissions
Gas	28.8
Private cars	26.9
Electricity	23.7
International flights (non-business)	12.2
Other household fuels	5.1
Public transport	3.1
Domestic flights	0.01
TOTAL	99.8

It is important to bear in mind that the figures in the table are averages and that the relative contributions from different sources, as already discussed, will vary between and within the different income bands. Nevertheless, these figures are useful when considering where to target efforts to save emissions.

Summary

- Globally individuals are estimated to be responsible for 64 per cent of all carbon emissions.

- The richest countries and the richest people, not always in the richest countries, cause the most carbon emissions. The top ten per cent of emitters live on all continents, with as many as one third of them from emerging countries.

- There is potential for individuals or groups to contribute significantly to cutting global emissions.

- In the UK it has been estimated that households are responsible for 61 per cent of all emissions.

- A relatively small number of individuals contribute disproportionately to the UK's emissions by flying long distances.

- A simple calculation suggests that feasible energy savings by households could reduce the UK's emissions by around 12 per cent.

- In UK households the main emissions are, in decreasing order, from the use of gas, cars, electricity and international non-business flights.

CHAPTER 4: YOUR CARBON FOOTPRINT AND HOW TO MEASURE IT

"... carbon emissions are implicated in almost every aspect of our lives."
Adam Corner & Jamie Clarke, *Talking Climate*, palgrave macmillan, 2016.

Getting personal

Before we, as individuals, can reduce the carbon emissions that arise both directly and indirectly from our use of energy and our consumption of goods and services we need to be able to measure, or at least closely estimate, our personal consumption of energy. It is often said that if you cannot measure something you cannot manage it and this is as true of greenhouse gas emissions as of anything else. Our use of energy covers a very wide spectrum from central heating, cooking and using electrical appliances in our homes, to driving cars, using public transport and flying, and to the embodied energy involved in the production of the food we eat and the manufacture of appliances and clothing that we buy, to name but a few. I am not going to propose that you turn yourself into a technical nerd who measures energy every time you use it but there are some simple but important things which you can do.

I am going to show ways in which you can estimate your emissions from different sources that can be accurately measured. This will help you to measure reductions in your emissions as you make changes to your home, means of getting about or lifestyle. It doesn't matter too much whether the calculations are completely accurate but it is essential that you stick with the same method of calculating them over a number of months or years, including looking back at your past energy consumption if you have the information to hand. Only then will you be able to compare like with like and to see how much progress you are making.

Necessarily this means that emissions from sources that are not easy, or even possible, to quantify will get missed out. In these cases being more aware of the impact of emissions involved in providing food or manufacturing clothing and appliances, for example, is likely to help you to reduce emissions in these areas as well.

Measuring electricity and gas consumption

Let's start in the home. We all have an electricity meter and many of us have a gas meter too.[171] Our energy company or companies read these meters several times a year and at other times they estimate the meter reading. This is not a very satisfactory way to get to understand your energy use although the numbers that appear on bills will provide an estimate of your annual electricity or gas consumption. But what we are after here is to get a feel quite quickly for how changes in our behaviour can affect our consumption. If your meter is hard to read because it is inaccessible or hard to reach then you can ask for it to be moved to a better location or changed; this can be done for free under some circumstances.[172]

Some bills unhelpfully refer to 'units' of energy but what we need to obtain from an electricity or gas meter is a measure of the kilowatt.hours consumed; this is usually abbreviated to kWh. A watt is a unit of power named after the Scottish engineer James Watt (1736-1819). Electrical power is the rate at which energy is used by an appliance such as a 50 watt (50 W) loud speaker or a two kilowatt (2 kW; kilo means a thousand) storage heater. Energy is calculated as the power of a device multiplied by the hours it has been used. So an old-fashioned 100 W light bulb left on continuously for ten hours will consume 1000 watt.hours (or 1 kWh) of energy. It is better to think in terms of kWh than 'units' as we'll discover later when converting kWh to the equivalent amount of CO_2 emitted.

Perhaps you could start by reading your meter(s) on the first day of every month and recording the readings in a notebook or on a spreadsheet. That way if you change something, other things being equal, you can tell within a month or two what effect it has had (or even sooner with weekly readings). If you have an Economy 7 meter, as well as a standard electricity meter, just read both meters and add together the amounts consumed.

Economy 7 electricity is not only cheaper but generally off-peak electricity also causes less emissions per kWh (it is said to be less carbon intensive). The carbon intensity of electricity varies during the day. At times of high electricity demand, at the start of the working day and in the early evening, more gas and coal are used to generate electricity, in addition to nuclear and renewables, thereby increasing the carbon intensity and *vice versa*.[173] The minimum intensity occurs around six o'clock in the morning. The daily range of carbon intensities is less in winter when demand is higher for most of the day. Therefore you can notionally minimise, but not easily quantify, your emissions by using off-peak electricity for running appliances such as dishwashers and washing machines at night. You don't have to have an Economy 7 connection to do this. The carbon intensity of UK electricity is monitored by at least two web sites in real time.[174]

Obviously there will be fluctuations in your energy consumption because, for all sorts of reasons, our lives do not usually follow the same pattern from day to day and so it is better to choose a minimum interval between meter readings, such as a week, that smooths out most of these fluctuations.

However, there is one special situation where it is worth taking electricity meter readings close together. Most homeowners would expect their overnight electricity consumption to be close to zero except for energy consumed by a fridge, freezer, fish tank or alarm system or anything else that operates 24 hours a day. So if you read the meter just before going to bed and as soon as you get up in the morning and take the difference in readings you will be able to estimate your 'baseload' consumption, that is what you consume continuously all year round. To estimate your annual baseload within 100 kWh you will need to make each meter reading to the nearest tenth of a kWh (the first number after the decimal point). This will be an important number because there are 8760 hours in a year! For example, if your overnight consumption is 1 kWh over eight hours then you will be consuming around 1100 kWh in a year equivalent to emitting around 0.55 tonnes of CO_2![175] This is a neat way of detecting all those appliances that still consume electricity while they are left on stand-by or which have been forgotten while plugged in to some inaccessible wall socket. Seek them out and disconnect them, then repeat the experiment to see how low you can get your overnight consumption. In our own home we've managed to cut our baseload to around 300 kWh per year, excluding the fridge-freezer, which is equivalent to about 35 watts running continuously or consuming 0.28 kWh overnight.

You may even want to find out how much electricity any particular appliance consumes especially if, like a fridge or a freezer, it is one that repeatedly cycles On and Off. To do this you can buy a handy device called either an energy monitor, power meter or watt-hour meter. This is a small meter costing around £20 which has a 13 amp socket, for the device to be measured, and a 13 amp plug for a mains socket and a small display screen. Simply plug the meter into the mains and plug the device into the meter's socket. The meter can give you an instantaneous measure of power being used or measure how much energy is consumed over a number of hours. It can pay for itself in terms of energy saved very quickly.

The types of electricity and gas meters mentioned above are gradually being overtaken by new technology in the form of smart meters. Energy companies in the UK have been told by the government to install a smart meter in every customer's home by 2020, although you can decline to have one if you wish.[176] As the government web site says *"Smart meters are the next generation of gas and electricity meters and they can offer a range of intelligent functions. For example, they can tell you how much energy you are using through a display in your home. They can also communicate directly with your energy supplier meaning that no one will need to come and read your meter in future. Most of the smart meters that are being installed today use mobile phone-type signals to send meter readings to your supplier, and other wireless technologies to send information to the in-home display."*[177] This means that, if you have a smart meter already, then you could have ignored the two previous paragraphs. The in-house display will tell you how much electricity (or gas) your home is using at any time. This should make it relatively easy to measure your baseload, to track down the consumption of individual appliances, by simply turning them Off and On again in turn, and to track down those appliances which you had imagined were turned Off.

Measuring fuel consumed for heating and cooking

Following the discovery of large reserves of natural gas in the North Sea a grid of pipelines was constructed in the 1970s and early 1980s across the UK to connect many houses to a gas main. Nevertheless it is easy to forget that not all homes in the UK are connected to mains gas and so are unable to use gas for heating and cooking. There are many regions, such as the South-West, Wales and large parts of Scotland, where fewer than 70 per cent of households are connected to mains gas. Households without gas use a variety of fuels for heating and cooking.

Homes that use burning oil (kerosene) for heating simply need to record the volume of fuel that they consume. Domestic oil pipelines from storage tanks can be fitted with a fuel flow meter but these tend to be expensive (costing well over £100). The much less accurate alternative is to use a sight tube on the outside of a tank. It will probably be very difficult to accurately monitor fuel consumption over periods of less than a few weeks with such a device.

Homes that use bottled gas (propane or butane as liquefied petroleum gas - LPG) for cooking will also have difficulty in monitoring their fuel consumption other than by checking the pressure or the level of liquid gas. In this situation it would seem that the best solution is simply to monitor how long a full bottle of gas lasts. You can then estimate the annual consumption by dividing the amount of gas in the full bottle by the number of days that the gas bottle lasted and then multiplying the resulting number by 365. LPG is currently the fossil fuel with the lowest emissions for households not on mains gas. It emits 23 per cent less CO_2 and other greenhouse gases than burning oil.[178]

Only one per cent of UK households used coal in 2014. Coal is sold by weight in sacks and the weight consumed seems to be the only way to estimate carbon emissions. It should be said that coal is one of the dirtiest of fossil fuels and its continued use should not be encouraged. However some coal products are now blended with renewable material and are said to produce up to 40 per cent less CO_2 emissions.[179]

If wood, as logs or pellets, is used from a sustainable supply then burning it will cause close to net zero emissions because the emissions from burning the wood will be offset by the absorption of CO_2 by the growing trees planted to replace the wood fuel. Nevertheless it should be recognised that this argument involves a time delay in absorbing CO_2 as far as trees planted to replace a particular load of logs are concerned because it takes a tree several decades to grow to maturity. However the use of a sustainable supply of wood should imply a continuous process of harvesting and planting trees over many years so that effectively there is no delay in absorbing CO_2 because it is going on all the time. A small amount of carbon emissions will have been caused by the equipment used to plant and harvest the trees, convert them into logs or pellets and transport them to your home. These can be classed as hard-to-measure indirect emissions. The wood must have been properly dried and ideally be burnt efficiently in a special stove.

The relative energy intensities and emissions of different fuels.[180]

Fuel	Energy intensity		Emissions
	(kWh per tonne)	(kWh per litre)	(kg CO_2e per kWh)
Kerosene	12,830	10.26	0.24666
Liquefied petroleum gas	13,710	7.01	0.21458
Coal	8,370		0.34129
Wood*	4,400		

*average depending on fuel type and water content

Measuring water consumption

Surprisingly, water has a carbon footprint. This may come as a surprise since basically it is a free resource that falls out of the sky, quite literally! But energy has to be used to pump water from boreholes, rivers or reservoirs into local reservoirs or water towers from which it flows downhill to our homes. It also has to be treated so as to be safe to drink. Once the used water enters drains and sewers it also has to be cleaned before it can be returned to the environment and this too requires energy.

Actually the footprint is quite small; each year an average two-person UK household will cause the emissions of only 38 kg CO_2e for the supplied water and 78 kg CO_2e for subsequent water treatment.[181,182] Although mains water is metered, so that we pay for what we actually use, many water meters are buried under the street or pavement and can be very inaccessible. For example, to get to my meter I have to get down on my hands and knees on the pavement outside the house, lever the cover up with a screwdriver and clean off the meter glass. Needless to say I don't read my water meter that often! Fortunately there are moves afoot to replace traditional meters with Automated Meter Readers (AMR) which transmit readings by radio to passing utility company vehicles. Eventually, we are told by United Utilities, *"..the new AMR technology means you will soon be able to log on to a dedicated page of our website."*[183] For now the most practical way to monitor water use is to rely on your six-monthly water bills.

There is one further aspect of water meters which is worth mentioning and that is to use them to check for water leaks provided that you can safely access your meter. Most water boards provide meters that as well as showing black numbers, representing cubic metres, display red numbers and dials representing fractions of a cubic meter (typically to a hundredth of a cubic meter which is equivalent to ten litres). You would have to have a really bad leak or monitor water usage over several days without any other water usage to detect a leak with this sort of meter. However AMR meters are already fitted by some companies such as Southern Water. These meters are very sensitive and can be read to the nearest fiftieth of a litre or 20 cubic centimetres! They also have a tell-tale disc with black and white segments which reacts to even smaller flows by a small rotation so that it is possible to immediately tell if water is flowing through the meter when, for example, the main stopcock of your home has been firmly closed. In the latter case you could check from time to time, perhaps overnight, whether you have a leak between the meter and your stopcock. If you suspect a leak in the home, then you could also check the meter when the home has been unoccupied for a day or more provided you are sure that there are no dripping taps, showers, cisterns or other ways that water is escaping. Checking for leaks is yet another way to minimise your carbon footprint, provided the leak can be located and repaired.

Measuring emissions from cars

Having considered electricity, gas and other fuels used for heating and cooking, and water, probably the next easiest source of CO_2 emissions to measure for most people is that from their cars. For some years all new petrol and diesel cars sold in the UK have had to be advertised with their fuel consumption in miles per gallon and litres of fuel per 100 km. The figures are given for urban driving, extra-urban driving and as a combination of the two. If you know how many miles you have driven, say in a year, and the nominal fuel consumption in miles per gallon (mpg) for the make and exact model of your car, then simply dividing the miles by the mpg will give you the amount of fuel consumed in gallons. A fixed amount of CO_2 is emitted by burning a gallon of petrol or diesel. Of course if you own a purely electric or hybrid car the electricity required to charge the battery will have been metered elsewhere (if not at home then keep a record of the electricity used). For a hybrid car the emissions from burning petrol or diesel also have to be taken into account and you will need to record the amount of fuel you consume.

But in the wake of the scandal in 2015 concerning cheating over nitrogen oxide (NO_x) and particulate matter emissions from diesel cars of the Volkswagen Group[184] how reliable are the CO_2 figures provided by the manufacturers (and, if you live in the UK, used to be displayed on your annual vehicle tax reminder letter from the Driver and Vehicle Licensing Agency)? There is no suggestion that any manufacturer has cheated in the same manner over CO_2 emissions. On the other hand, the way in which the CO_2 emissions tests are conducted is certainly divorced from real world driving. Real world driving includes driving up and down hills, starting and stopping, braking and accelerating and possibly carrying loads and roof racks which cause aerodynamic drag. In 2015 a report commissioned by the Committee on Climate Change, which advises the UK government on reducing CO_2 emissions, acknowledged that there is *"evidence of a growing 'gap' between official and real-world driving CO_2 emissions for new cars"*. The reason is that there are many ways in which cars in the current official test (called the New European Driving Cycle; NEDC) can be adapted to minimise their fuel consumption. These adaptations are described as allowable *"tolerances and flexibilities"*. For example, it is permissible to remove roof rails and the passenger door mirror, to reduce drag, and to increase tyre pressures above recommended values to reduce the rolling resistance of the tyres.[185] Many car advertisements now explicitly acknowledge that the NEDC produces results which are divorced from reality.

Until recently the gap between test results and real-world driving was considered to be 15 per cent on average, i.e. manufacturers' emissions figures were 15 per cent too low.[186] But in autumn 2015 this gap had reached 35 per cent for new cars, depending on the make and model, and was expected to grow.[187] So in reality, lacking detailed information about each model of car, it would be sensible to add up to 35 per cent when calculating the actual emissions. Hopefully this situation will be improved when the much more stringent Worldwide Harmonised Light Vehicles Test is introduced in 2017 in the EU. If you want to see how your emissions are decreasing the important thing, as explained later in this chapter, is to make the calculations in a consistent way so the actual mpg figure you use is not too important provided you recognise that it may change if you change your car.

Estimating emissions from flying

Globally, in 2005, flying created 2.4 per cent of all greenhouse gas emissions and in 2013 it caused 12 per cent of all CO_2 emissions from transport.[188] The intergovernmental Organisation for Economic Co-operation and Development has said that the aviation industry is *"one of the fastest growing in terms of its greenhouse gas emissions"*. For many better-off people flying can, probably unwittingly, be their largest source of emissions. For example, if you take a return economy flight from London to Johannesburg you will cause emissions of 3.5 tonnes of CO_2; London to Miami is 2.4 tonnes. This may be a big surprise but it is a well-kept secret which airlines, not surprisingly, are mostly unwilling to mention to their passengers. The large emissions are because of the very large distances flown, long-haul flights are typically thousands of kilometres long, and because the global warming effect of a commercial jet flying at an altitude of around 33,000 feet (ten kilometres) is considerably more than that from the emitted CO_2 alone. Water vapour in the exhaust can lead to the production of condensation trails (contrails) and emitted aerosols (very fine particles suspended in the air) may induce the growth of cirrus clouds, both of which trap heat in the atmosphere. There are other exhaust gases which also contribute to global warming. At present the UK government recommends that the CO_2 emissions should be multiplied by a factor of 1.9 (this is called the carbon dioxide multiplier) to fully account for their warming impact but even this does not take account of the unknown effect of induced cirrus clouds. I'll return to this topic in Chapter 8 but for now you need to make a note of all your non-business flights.[189]

Calculating your carbon footprint

Before discussing carbon footprints I should explain why it is necessary to convert measurements of kWh into emissions of CO_2. The reason is that some energy sources produce more carbon emissions per kWh than others. For example, because centralised power stations and the national grid are relatively inefficient (only about one-third of the energy consumed at a power station reaches consumers), generating a kilowatt.hour of electricity causes around 2.7 times as much CO_2 to be produced as when natural gas is burnt to produce a kilowatt.hour of heat energy in a boiler or gas ring in a home.[190] This is an average ratio for 2015; the precise ratio clearly would have varied as the power station fuel mix changed with the time of day and even during the year. By estimating CO_2 emissions all the energy consumption figures are translated to a common unit; after all, it is the carbon emissions that really count in the fight to mitigate climate change.

A carbon footprint is the total amount of greenhouse gases emitted in a fixed period, usually a year, by an individual, household or business. The UK average carbon footprint in 2005, including estimates of imports and international aviation and shipping, was 13.4 tonnes of CO_2e per person.[191] However if the UK's consumption emissions in 2013 are divided by the UK's mid-2013 estimate of population we find an even larger figure of 16.4 tonnes CO_2e.[192] As already mentioned, a footprint can comprise emissions from the direct use of energy (from energy sources that are easily measured) and from indirect uses (from energy sources which are harder or impossible to measure and often have to be estimated or inferred). We have now reached the stage where you know about your direct energy consumption. You will have established how much electricity, gas and water you used in the home, how many miles you drove and the details of the non-business flights, if any, you took in a year. Armed with this information you can now calculate your carbon footprint from direct emissions.

But before taking that step we need to consider exactly what sort of emissions we are trying to estimate. As we've seen, CO_2 is the most important greenhouse gas but there are also circumstances where the contributions of the gases methane (i.e. natural gas) and nitrous oxide are also important because their contributions to global warming are 28 and 265 greater, respectively, than the same volume of CO_2 alone over 100 years.[193] For this reason, and for completeness, emissions are usually expressed as carbon dioxide equivalent. This figure means the amount of CO_2 that would have the same effect on global warming as the CO_2 and all the other greenhouse gases that were emitted. It is usually expressed as kilograms or tonnes of carbon dioxide equivalent, written as CO_2e, and this is the unit that I shall use from here on.

We also want to come up with calculations of our emissions so that we can identify percentage or relative reductions in future. In other words consistency of calculation, meaning sticking with the same method, over several months or years is vital. Absolute values are less important to establish how our actions have helped us to cut our emissions.

Next we have to decide how to convert the energy measurements we've made into CO_2e emissions. We have a choice either to use one of a myriad of online footprint calculators or to do the calculations ourselves using a spreadsheet that takes account of the official set of conversion factors published each year by the former Department of Energy and Climate Change Affairs (DECC).[194,195] Some of these conversion factors change slightly from year to year. An obvious example is the conversion factor for electricity. This depends on the mix of fuels used in UK power stations (coal, gas or nuclear), the origins of any imported electricity and the proportion of electricity added to the grid from low-carbon renewable sources. This factor fluctuates from year to year but since 2005 it has mostly been on a downward trend as more renewable, implying low-carbon, sources have been included. So this can make a DIY calculation a bit tricky (but see later) and it requires some understanding of what is involved.

Online carbon footprint calculators

One has to treat online carbon footprint calculators with care. I checked over 20 online calculators and found only one that would give accurate, separate calculations of carbon emissions from each of the sources discussed previously which agreed with my own calculations using official DECC conversion factors. Many sites ask general questions about one's home and lifestyle which, although useful, do not address our immediate need. Others make inappropriate assumptions about what to include in the calculation, or offered calculations limited to only a few energy sources, or were designed to calculate ecological footprints and not carbon footprints, or simply didn't work! In addition it's very easy to locate any number of free smartphone apps by searching the internet but do be aware that they too may pose the same problems as the online calculators already mentioned.

Many sites offer facilities to pay money with which to offset the user's carbon emissions. The practicalities, and indeed morality, of offsetting are addressed later in this chapter.

The one online site that I found to match our needs was that run by the National Energy Foundation at www.carbon-calculator.org.uk/. The site was actually designed for small businesses but is equally suitable for households. It uses the correct conversion factors for electricity and gas in 2014 and 2015,[196] it requests the type of car used from a choice of nine (or alternatively the amount of fuel consumed)[197] and allows for several other modes of transport too.

The NEF site similarly asks about flights but unfortunately doesn't differentiate between longer and shorter long-haul flights. I suggest that this limitation can be simply got round by using a separate web site that takes great care to calculate accurate aircraft emissions for a given route; this is www.atmosfair.de/en which is very easy to use and allows the user to enter the airports visited, the class of seat and even the type of aircraft, if known.[198] Unfortunately it uses a carbon dioxide multiplier (sometimes called the radiation forcing index) of 3 whereas the UK government recommends 1.9 (the reasons for applying this multiplier were explained earlier in the chapter). This means that the emissions from the atmosfair site will need to be multiplied by 0.63 (1.9/3) to be consistent with the 1.9 multiplier.[199]

Looking beyond calculating just the emissions from electricity, gas, road fuel and flying there are useful sites which ask questions to help gauge your likely emissions from indirect sources too. These are necessarily less accurate but help you to compare your total emissions against other people's emissions if you are so inclined. Perhaps the best of these sites is at www.reap-petite.com/ which was created by a branch of the Stockholm Environment Institute (SEI) based in the University of York in the UK. SEI is a renowned independent international research institute which recently celebrated its 25th anniversary. The REAP-petite questionnaire not only asks about energy consumption but also about food, travel, shopping and other activities. It ends with optional questions about your views on environmental matters. Using this calculator you can experiment with calculating the effects of different changes to your home and lifestyle on your footprint.

The REAP-petite calculator also takes account of the number of children in a household by assuming that their emissions are the same as an adult's. It is tricky to determine what influence children have on a household's emissions. One might

80

automatically assume that children have a smaller carbon footprint than adults. Children don't drive cars but, at least in some better-off households, they are often driven to and from various activities including school. Children grow rapidly and will need larger clothes more frequently than adults wear out their own clothes. In addition, a friend with young children reminds me that children's clothes and bedding may need washing as much as three to six times more often. The parents of very young children may find that they need to wash their own clothes more often too. Also older children may occupy their own space in some homes and this may lead to extra demands for heating, lighting and entertainment equipment. So it is not altogether obvious that the presence of children will necessarily lead to a smaller per head carbon footprint in a household. Indeed one survey of electricity consumption in several hundred households in the city of Leicester, UK found that homes with either one or two teenagers were over three times more likely to be high consumers than if no teenager was present![200] The authors of the survey suggest that *"children and teenagers are perhaps less conscious of the electricity they use because they are disconnected from the financial implications of higher electrical energy demand."* I can hear many parents of teenagers agreeing with that statement.

As important for the determination of the household's footprint caused by direct emissions is what happens when a young person, or indeed any member of the household, is absent, say through studying or work, for a significant period. In this case it would seem to be best to either restrict footprint comparisons to when the household is complete or to estimate the annual footprint by extrapolating from such periods of a full household to a complete year. If the whole household is away on holiday for roughly the same length of time and month each year it will not be necessary to make allowances for that when making comparisons between different years.

The DIY footprint calculation

For anyone happy to work with figures it is perhaps simpler, and even more satisfying, to calculate your emissions yourself. If you prefer to use an online calculator you can skip this section.

As already described, the basic equation for electricity, gas and other energy sources is,

Emissions (kg CO_2e) = energy used (kWh) x energy conversion factor (kg CO_2e/kWh)

Energy conversion factors for 2015 from DECC (www.gov.uk/government/collections/government-conversion-factors-for-company-reporting) or the National Energy Foundation (NEF; www.carbon-calculator.org.uk/) are given in the table.

Emissions factors for household energy and water consumption in 2015

Energy source or water used	Energy conversion factor	Units of conversion factor
Electricity	0.50035	kg CO_2e/kWh
Mains gas	0.18445	kg CO_2e/kWh
LPG	*1.50938	kg CO_2e/litre gas
Coal	*3.065	kg CO_2e/kg coal
Kerosene	*2.53215	kg CO_2e/litre oil
Water supplied	0.344	kg CO_2e/cubic metre
Sewerage treatment	0.708	kg CO_2e/cubic metre

*Conversion factors from the NEF web site www.nef.org.uk/. Other factors from DECC.[194]

The two figures for water refer to water supplied to the home and to the treatment of sewerage. Water bills usually provide an estimate of sewerage as a percentage of water supplied.

The relevant conversion factor for natural gas can be found on the DECC conversion-factor web site mentioned earlier in this section by clicking on the Fuels tab and looking for Natural gas in the Gaseous fuels table. The Gross CV value for 2015 is 0.18445 kg CO_2e per kWh. Gross CV, which DECC recommends to be used over Net CV, stands for the total Calorific Value or heating value derived from the gas. Thus calculating emissions from mains natural gas is straightforward. At present only a very few UK energy companies add small amounts of so-called green gas to the grid. Green gas is a renewable (non-fossil fuel) resource. It is derived from biogas produced by anaerobic digesters, which use organic waste of various sorts to generate methane, the principal component of natural gas. This means that in principle emissions from burning 100 per cent green gas can essentially be ignored. However, it is not easy to allow for the possibly uncertain amount of green gas in your supply and so conservatively it is best to use the Gross CV value mentioned above.

As already discussed, actual car emissions can be estimated from miles driven or fuel consumed. A fixed volume of fuel when burnt will emit a fixed amount of CO_2 so if we know the appropriate conversion factor we can calculate how much CO_2 was emitted by driving so many miles. DECC reports conversion factors of 2.1944 and 2.5839 kg CO_2e per litre for petrol and diesel, respectively. This gives us two equations:

CO_2 emissions (kg) = 9.98 x (miles driven)/(average miles per gallon) for petrol cars and

CO_2 emissions (kg) = 11.75 x (miles driven)/(average miles per gallon) for diesel cars.

Average miles per gallon for your car are best estimated from the mpg display on your dashboard, if you have this option, since we know that manufacturers' figures are inflated and are not based on real world driving. Even this mpg figure has been shown to be a few per cent higher than estimates based on fuel bought and miles driven but some small discrepancy is to be expected because of other factors.[201]

But, if you record how much fuel you buy and the miles driven using that fuel you'll get an even more accurate mpg figure (but see next paragraph).

Alternatively, if you prefer to record only the amount of fuel your car used, including if you have a hybrid car, you can use whichever of the two following equations is appropriate,

CO_2 emissions (kg) = 2.194 x (litres of fuel consumed) for petrol (and hybrid) cars and

CO_2 emissions (kg) = 2.584 x (litres of fuel consumed) for diesel (and hybrid) cars.

The calculations for cars provide emissions in CO_2. Emissions of methane and nitrous oxide can be ignored since cars emit so little of these gases.

Flight emissions are best calculated as described in the previous section. Remember to multiply emissions figures from the atmosfair web site by 0.63.

This brief section has therefore provided you with all the information you need to calculate the carbon footprint of yourself or your household on your own without using a web site.

Offsetting carbon emissions[202]

Carbon offsetting is sometimes suggested as a method of reducing the carbon footprints of individuals or organisations. Rather than the emitters having to reduce their greenhouse gas emissions, offsetting involves someone else reducing their emissions instead, usually for a payment. The idea is that the cost of offsetting, if priced realistically, will provide an incentive to reduce emissions.

Offsetting is often mentioned in the context of extra or 'unavoidable' emissions over and above a given lifestyle that, with more care or restraint, could be avoided. For example, you might pay someone in a developing country to plant trees that are intended to eventually soak up at least the same amount of emissions that you will cause by taking a holiday flight. Other offsetting projects include the development of hydro-electric power stations, biomass-fuelled combined heat and power plant and wind farms where more carbon-intensive power generation would otherwise have taken place.

However, there are several problems with offsetting schemes. The purchaser needs to be sure that,

- the emissions reductions from their chosen scheme would not have happened anyway (otherwise their emissions will not actually have been offset)
- the scheme will cause a permanent reduction in emissions
- the scheme has not caused an increase in emissions elsewhere
- the scheme will remove greenhouse gases at broadly the same time and rate as they are emitted otherwise, on balance, the emissions could end up causing a net increase, even if temporarily, in atmospheric CO_2.

There is also a moral question to be considered about using offsetting schemes in developing countries. Why should someone who is much poorer than we are in the UK or another developed country be encouraged to help reduce emissions so that we can continue to live in an unsustainable and even extravagant way? Logically, if we take responsibility for our own emissions, we should end up offsetting our own extra and 'unavoidable' emissions by our own actions. For example, if we feel we have to buy a new car which is larger than what we really need, maybe we should offset the extra emissions involved by turning down our central heating at home until the equivalent emissions have been saved! Or we should take a high-speed train to go on holiday to the Mediterranean instead of taking that transatlantic flight to the Caribbean.

The UK government recommends that offsetting should only be considered after the emitter has quantified the likely emissions involved, considered all actions to avoid the emissions and taken steps to reduce the emissions by efficiency measures. Therefore offsetting should be considered only as a last resort, after we have reduced our emissions as much as we can. Nevertheless, some non-business travel (and even other activities) may be judged to be truly unavoidable for a variety of reasons. In these cases, individuals may wish to buy assured offset credits from a regulated scheme that ensures that the corresponding emissions reductions elsewhere in the world are both additional and permanent.[203]

If it works as intended, offsetting can lead to carbon neutral actions with zero net emissions. Ideally, this is achieved, as described above, through a transparent process of calculating emissions, minimising those emissions and then offsetting residual emissions. However, offsetting is not a 'cure' for climate change. There is no doubt that in this context the most effective way to combat climate change is to reduce our personal emissions. There are many actions we can take that do not necessarily result in a less comfortable lifestyle, just in a more intelligent one that recognises the impact that individual actions can have on the world.

Summary

- *Home owners can learn to understand and reduce their energy consumption through reading their electricity, gas and water meters and taking simple actions.*
- *Likewise they can calculate their carbon emissions from electricity, gas, car(s) and air travel using a simple online web site, a spreadsheet or pen and paper calculations.*
- *Carbon offsetting is not a viable strategy in most cases.*
- *The most effective way we can individually combat climate change is to reduce our personal emissions. There are many things we can do that do not result in a less comfortable lifestyle, just in a more intelligent one.*

CHAPTER 5: ACTIONS THAT WILL HELP YOU CUT YOUR CARBON EMISSIONS

I have now covered the reasons for saving energy and explained how by doing so your carbon footprint and personal contribution to climate change will be reduced. I have also covered the measurements you need to make to monitor your direct use of energy and how these measurements can be turned into estimates of carbon emissions. So now we can begin to consider some practical actions that will help you reduce your carbon footprint.

Three steps to follow

There are three separate steps to follow which logically should be considered in order when considering how to save energy and when making a plan to reduce your carbon footprint. These are the top three components of what is called the energy hierarchy. In the following chapters I shall discuss these steps in turn as applied to the three main activities that contribute to our direct use of energy; these activities are using electricity, heat and transport.

The first step is simply to **lessen your energy demand**. This can often be done by changes in behaviour alone which, although at first they may be hard to follow consistently, can have zero cost attached. This is a good way to start on the road to cutting your carbon emissions. A simple example is turning down the room thermostat on a central heating system and putting on an extra layer of clothing if consequently you feel too cool. There are lots of other suggestions in the next three chapters which you can 'pick and mix' according to your own circumstances. It is worth emphasising strongly that it is far better to avoid emitting carbon dioxide in the first place than to depend on nature or even technology to remove it from the atmosphere later, even assuming this is practical.

The second step is to **use energy more efficiently**. By using energy more efficiently you should consume less energy yet achieve the same required outcome. For example, insulating a loft will reduce the loss of heat through the roof, probably make the home warmer and lead to a lower consumption of energy and consequent production of greenhouse gas emissions. But there will be some cost attached to doing this for both materials and, if you don't do it yourself, for labour. This is where those who are better off can make a strong personal contribution to mitigating climate change.

Another option to use energy more efficiently is clearly to replace an old appliance with a new, more efficient one. Many appliances are becoming more efficient in their use of energy as technology advances and as the pressures from legislation take effect. But learning of the rapid advances in these areas should not automatically dictate that you go out and buy the latest model. The reason is the energy, and carbon emissions, involved in sourcing the raw materials and in the manufacture and transport of an item, particularly if the item we want to buy has been imported. These are often referred to as embedded or embodied emissions.

Just to give an extreme example, a large top of the range, petrol 4x4 car will cause the emission of 35 tonnes of CO_2 in its manufacture[204] and yet will deliver only around 32 miles per gallon. Thus, on average, the emissions from driving this car will not exceed the embodied emissions until the car has been driven for 112,000 miles! In contrast, a Citroen C1 car has embodied emissions of around 6 tonnes and can deliver around 65 miles per gallon so its tailpipe emissions will exceed its embodied emissions after driving only 39,000 miles.[204] In other words the embodied emissions of a vehicle, or even an appliance or a computer, can be very significant when compared to the emissions from its daily use.

To decide what to do one needs to know the embodied and operational emissions in each case which is not always easy. Further, a well used appliance may no longer be as efficient as it was when new; it may, as a result of normal wear and tear, use more electricity for example. There may also be some situations where upgrading an item will save more carbon than replacing it. Almost the only circumstances in which it is worth replacing an appliance from the environmental point of view is when it is beyond repair or becomes unreliable or unsafe. Even in this situation it is often worth considering buying a second-hand replacement and giving away your old appliance to someone who might find some value in it. This will avoid the embodied emissions of a new item.

Lastly, the third step relates to **generating your own energy**. Other than using a diesel generator, which obviously I do not recommend because it likely uses a fossil fuel, this means installing some form of renewable energy source such as photovoltaic panels which produce electricity. Clearly this incurs a greater financial outlay and should only be considered once you have taken the first two steps to maximise reductions and efficiencies in energy use. In fact, if you are going to apply for some grants to help you take this third step, you will usually have to show that you have completed the first two steps anyway. Again, these are opportunities to be seized by the better off who can afford the relevant capital investment.

So in summary, we need to aim for Less demand for energy, Efficient use of energy and Generating our own energy. I call this the LEG system; these are the legs that we will use to enable us to take the steps along the road to our shrinking footprint!

In the next three chapters I shall offer suggestions for how the three different steps mentioned above can be applied in turn to the use of electricity in the home, to the use of heat in the home and to how we get about and travel. It is up to you, the reader, to decide which measures to adopt to reduce your emissions and to form a plan of how and when to do so.

Waste and re-cycling

There remains one further area where energy can be saved and carbon emissions avoided in the sense that waste is a resource that can be used to prevent the unnecessary expenditure of energy. I have already mentioned using appliances for the longest possible time but eventually we are faced with the problem of how to dispose of a defunct item or waste in the form of food scraps, packaging and the other minutiae of daily life. In almost all circumstances, but depending on the services offered by local authorities, it is possible to re-cycle waste so that it can be turned into a new substance or product. Failing that, energy can be recovered from waste by various means. Finally, anything that remains is sent to landfill or is just burned without energy recovery. Landfill is to be avoided at all costs since the breakdown of organic matter in the waste by bacteria under anaerobic conditions leads to the creation of the powerful greenhouse gas methane which, if not captured and burned, can escape to the atmosphere.

Waste is collected either at the kerbside in wheelie bins or at household waste recycling centres. Kerbside waste collection may include waste in black bags, food in special containers and garden waste. Some of this waste may be sorted after collection but in other cases black bag waste is sent to an incinerator (or energy recovery facility) to be burned and generate electricity. Household waste recycling centres are a very efficient way of dealing with waste of all kinds because the waste can be loaded into different skips according to type and be taken off to be treated accordingly but users do need their own transport to access the centre.

91

In the ideal world of a circular economy all waste will be re-used. WRAP, the UK Waste and Resources Action Programme, says the circular economy aims to ensure that resources remain in use for as long as possible and the maximum value is extracted from these resources whilst in use, and then to recover and regenerate products and materials at the end of each service life. The arguments for a circular economy are to reduce waste, drive greater resource productivity, deliver a more competitive UK economy, position the UK to better address emerging resource security and scarcity issues in the future and to help reduce the environmental impacts of our production and consumption in both the UK and abroad.[205]

Summary

- *Personal carbon footprints are best reduced by taking the following three steps in the energy hierarchy in turn. These are the LEG procedures described above.*
  - *Step 1. Lessen demand for energy.*
  - *Step 2. Efficient energy use.*
  - *Step 3. Generate one's own energy.*
- *Waste is actually a resource that can be used in various ways to save energy.*
- *It is important, where applicable, to sort waste into the correct waste streams.*
- *Ideally the world will eventually move to a circular economy where all waste will be re-cycled.*

CHAPTER 6: ELECTRICITY IN THE HOME

As we saw in Chapter 3, on average in the UK almost a quarter of household emissions result from the consumption of electricity. We use electricity extensively throughout our homes. In fact, our dependence on electricity becomes all too apparent on those rare occasions when we suffer from a power cut. It is important to save electricity whenever we can simply because of the impact that the huge number of household consumers can have on the demand for electricity. There are many stories around the phenomenon of 'TV pick-up' meaning the surge in electricity demand that occurs when a popular TV programme finishes and viewers make for the kitchen to switch on a kettle for a nice cup of tea. Such a surge can be expressed as the output, temporarily, of several power stations. More prosaically this means that if most householders make an effort to turn off lights, or switch off appliances that are on stand-by, it can have a substantial effect on the national demand for electricity.

In the UK electricity is supplied mainly by the Big Six companies as they are often called (British Gas, EDF Energy, e-on, Npower, Scottish Power and SSE). These companies were set up when the energy sector was privatised in 1990. But since 1997 a number of smaller independent companies have entered the market to provide greater competition.

Carbon emissions from electricity consumption are determined by the proportions of primary energy used in power stations, such as coal and gas, and nuclear, renewable and imported energy. The relevant conversion factor, expressed in kg CO_2e per kWh, is published annually by DECC.[206] For example, the figure for 2016 is 0.41205 kg CO_2e per kWh. This number does not include losses in the transmission and distribution of electricity through the national grid. A figure covering these losses, which should be added to the first figure when calculating your emissions, is 0.03727 kg CO_2e per kWh. Be aware that electricity conversion factors change slightly from year to year as the energy mix varies.

Herein lies a problem, first mentioned in the Preface, because many companies offer options that include 'green' or renewable energy. You might well ask therefore, if you buy electricity from such a company, whether the conversion factor that you use and consequently your carbon footprint, should be less. Sadly the situation is more complex than that because under UK law, under what is called the Renewables Obligation, all electricity companies are mandated to include a percentage of renewable energy in their supply and this imposed percentage increases year on year. To satisfy the law, and Ofgem, the UK government's Office of Gas and Electricity Markets, who administer the scheme, the generating and supply companies buy and sell renewable electricity to meet the demands of their customers. In this situation there is no net emissions reduction advantage to the UK as a whole if you, the customer, buy electricity on a 'green' tariff from such a supplier. The only exception I can imagine is where a customer can truly say that they have bought zero-carbon electricity when the supplier supplies 100 per cent renewable energy all of which has been generated either by themselves or others (if all companies did this it is obvious that everyone could claim to use zero-carbon electricity; it seems to me that the argument is no less valid when applied to a single company). A very few companies claim this and they can be found at www.greenelectricity.org/. In this case I would suggest that when calculating your emissions you will only need to use the much smaller 'Transmission and distribution' conversion factor when calculating your footprint.

At least one company (Ecotricity) publishes the life cycle emissions per kWh of its electricity. This calculation takes account of emissions from 'cradle to grave' of each source of energy used to generate their electricity. Such calculations are not normally used, or are not available, when estimating a carbon footprint and can be ignored for our purposes; they only contribute about 1.5 per cent of the main electricity conversion factor anyway.

Suggested actions to save energy and greenhouse gas emissions follow using the three steps scheme described in Chapter 5. The use of electricity for heating is discussed in Chapter 7.

Step 1. Suggestions for reducing your electricity demand

The following Step 1 suggestions are for changes in behaviour that will save energy. Suggestions that involve some expenditure follow in Step 2.

• A universal example of electricity use in the home is **interior lighting**. The obvious way to reduce demand is simply to turn off all lights when leaving a room unoccupied and to use only the lights you need in each room.

• Some home owners like to leave on an **external light** at night either for security or to give a welcoming appearance to their home. In the former case this can be avoided entirely by fitting a passive infrared sensor (usually called a PIR sensor) which detects the approach of a warm body (whether human or four-legged) and will activate the light. This might prove a greater deterrent to an intruder than a light left on constantly. In the second case the light can and should be turned Off at bedtime. In rural locations bright external lights may be seen as a form of pollution, which disturbs wildlife, and as a nuisance by residents.

• **Appliances** are the next most obvious consumers of electricity in the home. Appliances include computers and their accessories, entertainment equipment and battery chargers. The aim here is to switch off all those appliances that otherwise would remain on stand-by all year round (remember there are 8760 hours in a year and 8760 times a small number can give quite a large number!). If you spend around £20 on an energy monitor or power meter (as mentioned in Chapter 4) you can quickly go around the house and check the consumption of each appliance in turn in its On, Standby and Off states. I can guarantee that **any device which is turned off at the wall will consume zero electricity**. If a wall socket is hard to reach or you prefer an even simpler solution there are wireless devices (smart plugs) which allow appliances plugged into mains sockets to be remotely switched off at the click of a button. Unfortunately on the continent of Europe mains-electricity wall sockets usually lack switches and in such cases the only solution is to unplug an appliance or to change the socket (switched wall sockets said to meet EU requirements can be bought in the USA).[207]

- There are some 'urban myths' around **computers and routers**. A screen saver doesn't actually save energy and may even use more energy and prevent the computer from going into hibernation. Putting a computer and its screen into hibernation will save some electricity but, if you can, always **switch them off at the wall** once your session has finished. Routers, whether wireless or not, don't have to be left on 24/7 (unless of course they also provide a landline phone connection). I've turned my non-wireless router off after each session for years without apparent harm. If you are uncertain, do an experiment and see what happens.

- **Fridges and freezers** necessarily consume electricity all year round. How long they are in their On state depends on their temperature setting and it is worth checking that this is not set at too low a temperature. Many fridges or freezers have a dial with numbers around the circumference; the higher numbers denote lower temperature settings but this doesn't help you to set the temperature to a particular value. To check that the temperature is not too low buy a cheap fridge/freezer thermometer for a few pounds. Ideally a fridge should be set between 3 and 5°C. Food stored in a freezer will last indefinitely if it is kept at around -18°C. Colder temperature settings will use more energy unnecessarily. Allow 24 hours for the temperature to stabilise after you've changed the temperature setting dial.

Other appliances include white goods such as washing machines, dish washers and tumble dryers which I shall discuss separately. It is arguable whether dishwashers and tumble dryers are in fact luxury items. There are some homes today without a dishwasher and where the tumble dryer is there for emergencies only and mostly gathers dust.

• There are simple procedures you can follow to minimise the energy consumption of a **washing machine**. Maybe 80 per cent or more of a washing machine's electricity consumption is for heating water so it is essential to minimise your use of hot water. The rules are: always wash a full load, choose the right programme for the articles being washed (including a fast wash if appropriate), use an economy cycle (which means the machine uses less water and electricity but the wash may take longer) and use detergents that allow the wash to proceed at the lowest possible temperature (even 30°C is feasible).

• Energy related arguments about whether to use a **dishwasher** tend to centre around how much hot water they use and whether the machine uses less hot water than washing up by hand. It is easy to win the argument by assuming that washing up by hand is done under a running hot water tap (but see below).[208] However these arguments overlook the additional embodied energy involved in the manufacture of the dishwasher. At least some dishwashers can be connected to a less energy intensive hot water supply, if you have one, but take advice before doing so.[209] The occupants of a home will need to make a judgement whether to buy a dishwasher or not depending on the number of people in the household, how frequently they wash the dishes and how much time they have for washing up by hand. My favourite washing up method by hand, which I have shown to use less water than a dishwasher, is the following. Wash up in a bowl in the sink. Rinse the dishes in running cold to lukewarm water while waiting for the hot water to arrive (if you have a combi boiler you'll need to do this under the cold tap). Run just enough water plus detergent into the bowl to wash the dishes and give surfaces that come into contact with food or liquids a quick rinse under the hot tap before draining them. Empty and refill the bowl as necessary if the water in the bowl gets too dirty. Finally rinse larger vessels (tea pots, saucepans etc.) with cold water and pour it over the cutlery in a separate draining basket. Leave items to dry overnight or dry up by hand. Job done. Incidentally, washing up in cold water is not usually recommended. Hot to warm water is required to melt fat or grease on dishes and improves the performance of detergents.[210]

- **Tumble dryers**[211] should only be used as a last resort. For example, if indoor drying areas are full up, the weather is too wet for an outdoor drying frame or washing line or in an 'emergency'. A tumble dryer is quite energy intensive so set it to run for a short period and check frequently on the contents, removing items as they dry. A friend tells me she hates ironing and so she tumble dries clothes for 5-8 minutes, just long enough to get rid of wrinkles and creases, before putting the clothes on a hanger. I suspect that this uses more electricity because an iron cycles On and Off as it is used (as well as giving clothes a final drying) whereas the tumble dryer uses electricity to heat a continuous stream of air as well as turning the drum. Some tumble dryers are designed to use mains gas instead of electricity to provide the heat that dries the clothes. For maximum efficiency consider using a dryer that uses 'heat pump technology'. Moisture is removed from warm damp air extracted from the drum before the air is re-heated and returned to the drum. This saves significant amounts of heat and therefore energy. Ensure the air filter remains unblocked for maximum efficiency. Obviously in a household with young children demand for drying may sometimes necessitate the frequent use of a tumble dryer but this is a habit worth dropping as soon as the demand declines. An airing cupboard with a hot water tank is a real boon for finishing off the drying, hence its name, but my wife tells me this is old-fashioned.

You will need to do a test with an energy monitor to determine whether each appliance consumes zero electricity when nominally switched off. Otherwise, assuming the wall sockets are accessible and visible, a quick check at bedtime each day can pick up any appliances unnecessarily left on. That could save around eight hours of consumption by each appliance for 365 days each year.

• One of the last topics to cover in this section is reducing the use of electricity in **cooking** whether in a microwave, on a hob or in an oven. A microwave oven is the most energy-efficient (it uses 60 to 80 per cent less energy than an oven)[212], followed by an electric hob and lastly an electric oven. There are some simple ways to save energy too. For example, measure out the water you need to make a drink when boiling a kettle, and only make toast in a toaster and not under the grill. Mike Berners-Lee, in his book *How bad are bananas?*, points out that adding milk to your tea or coffee triples its carbon footprint.[213] Many other suggestions to reduce electricity consumption by hobs and ovens can be found online. For example, you could cook larger quantities than you need for a single meal and save the rest, after it has cooled, in the fridge or freezer to quickly re-heat and eat later, you could turn off the oven around ten minutes before cooking is completed (it will keep hot for that long), you could use a pressure cooker for cooking pulses, and even joints of meat, whole meals or stews (food cooks faster in a pressure cooker), and a steamer for cooking layers of vegetables over a single ring.[214,212]

- **Outdoor appliances**. These so-called labour saving items are particularly wasteful of electricity in that in most cases using a bit of elbow grease will do the job just as well and the healthy exercise will be well within the capabilities of many people. I am referring of course to **leaf blowers, high-pressure washers, small chain saws, hedge and grass trimmers, shredders, rotivators and scarifiers**. There may be more. And wouldn't it be so much more enjoyable to be outdoors without having to put up with the noise of these devices from neighbouring gardens. Even **lawn mowers** can be replaced by a hand-propelled version which may even have been reconditioned.

- **Off-peak electricity**. Most people are aware that they can use cheaper off-peak electricity at night time. In the UK the electricity is usually sold on the Economy 7 tariff, meaning the electricity is available at a reduced cost for seven hours a night. The actual hours that are cheaper depend on your supplier and where you live. It is practical for some appliances, such as dishwashers, washing machines and even ovens, to use off-peak electricity to save money. However using off-peak electricity in the home will not save electricity - an appliance will use the same amount of electricity to perform its function whatever the time of day - but it is interesting to ask whether the resulting carbon emissions are less during the night hours. The answer will depend on how much electricity is being generated by burning coal or gas or is being supplied from nuclear power stations or renewables as explained in Chapter 4. In general the amount of CO_2 emitted per kWh tends to be less as night.

Step 2. Suggestions for using your electricity more efficiently

Step 2 provides suggestions for saving electricity which involve some expenditure.

• **Lighting.** Electrical shops agreed voluntarily with the UK government in 2009 to stop selling old fashioned, incandescent filament light bulbs because they are so inefficient and wasteful of energy. Halogen light bulbs are also incandescent and therefore inefficient. In the last few years the manufacturers of light bulbs have made tremendous strides in producing bulbs that are much more efficient and longer lasting too. First there were compact fluorescent lamps (CFLs) and now there are light-emitting diodes (LEDs). It is a good plan to change all your existing light bulbs to CFLs, or to the even more efficient **LEDs,** as and when they fail (or even earlier because replacing an old filament bulb with an LED could pay for itself within months). Aim to replace all your incandescent bulbs, both indoors and out, within a few years. Older strip lights can be replaced by the more efficient T4, T5 or T8 fluorescent tubes. Dimming modern lamps saves electricity and today even LEDs can be dimmed. LED bulbs can have different terminations (bayonet or screw) and come in different sizes to match most fittings, so choose your replacement carefully. CFLs and LEDs produce a whiter light which is described on the packaging as the colour 'temperature'. 3000K is a typical 'temperature' for a warm white colour; lower temperatures provide a more yellow to orange light and higher temperatures a more white to blue light. It is sensible to buy a single bulb to start with to see that you are happy with the new colour.

• **Appliances**, including white goods and computers, that are designed for the same job can differ widely in their energy consumption. When replacing a broken or worn out appliance, including buying a new one, look for the EU energy label (rated A to D) and buy the most efficient model that you can afford (typically A+ to A+++). It is worth remembering that a large efficient fridge, for example, could use more energy than a smaller less efficient one. Some models of white goods provide estimates of their energy usage in a year. Office equipment should display the Energy Star label. Other labels to look out for are the Energy Saving Trust Recommended and the European Ecolabel.

- A **washing machine** uses plenty of hot water and it used to be possible to buy machines with separate hot and cold fill connections. Today models that allow one to provide hot water from another less energy intensive source, such as a gas boiler or a solar panel, do not seem to exist;[215] the water is heated electrically in the appliance.

- If you want to use energy more efficiently in the kitchen there is a huge variety of **cooking equipment** to choose from but only replace what you already have when it is worn out or beyond repair because of the energy (and emissions) embodied in its manufacture. Electric (ceramic and induction) hobs have become very popular because they offer flat surfaces that are easier to clean and are said to have a more even distribution of heat than solid plate hobs. Induction hobs are also more electrically efficient than other electrically heated hobs but need to use special 'ferrous' pans. But any electrically based hob or oven will always cause the emissions of more CO_2 than the gas-based equivalent simply because gas is the cleaner fuel as already mentioned in Chapter 4. An electric oven causes the emissions of around 80 per cent more CO_2 than a gas oven and electric and induction hobs emit almost twice and 40 per cent more CO_2, respectively,[216] but check the latest figures before buying. If you buy a new oven look out for an EU Energy Label when making your choice; it is conceivable that a modern, well insulated electric oven will cause fewer emissions than an old, poorly insulated gas oven even though gas would be the better choice for a new oven. An interesting alternative option is to use a thermal cooker, the modern version of the 'hay box', in which food brought up to temperature slowly cooks in a highly insulated container.[217]

- **Voltage optimisation**. Today electricity in the UK is supplied at a standard 230±10% volts AC whereas previously the

UK standard was 240 volts AC. Thus the energy consumed by some appliances, mostly those that have motors such as fridges and freezers, can be saved by reducing the voltage to around 220 volts AC. This is called voltage optimisation. The measured savings can be quite small (one site reports a two per cent saving[218]) and the technique is probably more suitable for use in commercial premises which may have more motors, fans and pumps than a home.

Step 3. Generating your own electricity

Step 3 covers various forms of renewable energy.

The final energy saving step for electricity is to generate your own from a renewable source. A trivial example is the use of outdoor solar lights along paths and in gardens. But for most homes generating your own electricity will mean installing **photovoltaic (PV) panels** on the roof, although in principle panels could be sited at ground level. PV panels work on indirect or scattered sunlight as well as on direct sunlight. Ideally in the UK they should be sited on a 30° pitched, south-facing roof but orientations of even east or west will work too. The panels should not be shaded by trees, chimneys, dormer windows or other buildings and a skilled installer should be able to provide an accurate estimate of the effect of shading for different seasons and times of day. The panels are often connected in series and utilise a single inverter which converts the DC electricity from the panels to AC electricity suitable for consumption in the home or for passing to the grid. This means that if one panel is shaded it will badly affect the output of all the panels. It's a bit similar to a string of Christmas tree lights; if one light fails the whole string fails! However, the effects of shading can be minimised by using a micro-inverter on each panel. In this case each panel produces an AC voltage independently and shading of one panel has a minimal effect on the total AC output.

PV panels have lifetimes of 20-25 years and their efficiency drops off by about 0.5 per cent each year (implying a loss of 12 per cent over 25 years). PV panels also are less efficient the hotter they are. On average in the UK PV panels can be expected to deliver 10.4 per cent of their installed capacity in a year (this is because the Sun only shines in the daytime, is only close to its maximum intensity around midday and clouds reduce the sunlight reaching the panel). So, for example, a set of panels rated at a maximum power output of 1 kW might be expected to deliver 911 kWh of energy in a year (1 kW x 0.104 (10.4%) x 24 hours x 365 days = 911 kWh).

Unless a home has batteries to store electricity the output from PV panels either has to be used immediately (including heating water with an immersion heater) or it has to be fed into the national grid. So if a home is left unoccupied in the daytime during the week, for example, it will not always be possible to use much of the free electricity from the panels in the home. Domestic batteries that can store at least 2 kWh are an alternative solution and are now available commercially.[219] Such a battery is unlikely to meet the total annual needs of most homes but the point is that it makes having the PV panels seem more worthwhile. There is also a financial advantage in capturing much, if not all, of the output of a home's PV panels which otherwise would have to be exported to the national grid.

Unless your home is situated in an open and exposed location suitable for a **wind turbine**, or has access to a suitable stream or river to generate **hydroelectricity**, then PV panels will be your best bet for generating low-carbon renewable electricity.

How are you doing with reducing your electricity consumption?

It may provide encouragement to compare your electricity consumption with other homes in your postcode area and local authority area and, nationally, with similar-sized homes.

You can compare your annual electricity consumption with other domestic users in your complete postcode area as follows. Download the relevant Excel spreadsheet for 2013 from www.gov.uk/government/statistics/postcode-level-electricity-estimates-2013-experimental. DECC describes the data as experimental apparently because the methodology used to produce them is still under development. Use Find & Select > Find > Find Next to locate the entry for your postcode. Columns D and E give the mean (average) and median consumptions for your postcode. By definition there are as many homes with consumptions greater than the median value as less than it. If everyone was able to reduce their consumption to be less than the median in 2013 then overall consumption would decrease dramatically!

The average annual electricity consumption in different local authority areas is available at www.gov.uk/government/statistical-data-sets/regional-and-local-authority-electricity-consumption-statistics-2005-to-2011.

How are you doing with reducing your electricity consumption? (continued)

Download the file called 'Regional and local authority electricity consumption statistics: 2005 to 2014' as an Excel spreadsheet.

Click on the '2014r' tab at the bottom of the spreadsheet. Use Find & Select > Find > Find Next to locate the entry for your local authority. Columns R and S give mean (average) and median consumptions of Standard electricity and columns P and Q give mean (average) and median consumptions of Economy 7 electricity. To help you compare your consumption with similarly sized homes the following table gives median annual electricity consumptions for differently sized homes in England in 2011.

Home	Median annual electricity consumption (kWh)
Terraced house – mid-terrace	3,400
Terraced house – end-terrace	3,800
Semi-detached house	4,000
Detached house	4,600
Bungalow	2,900
Flat	2,800

Data from Table 2 in Hulme, Jack, Beaumont, Adele, and Summers, Claire. "Report 3: Metered Fuel Consumption: Including Annex on High Energy Users." BRE/DECC, December 2013. Table 2 also provides data on median consumption by dwelling age and floor area.

Summary

- *Emissions per kWh from 'green' electricity suppliers will depend on how the 'green' electricity was acquired and generated.*

- *Step 1. The demand for electricity in the home can be reduced by always switching off unnecessary lights, switching all appliances off at the wall (or unplugging them) when not in use, setting temperatures carefully on fridges and freezers, using cool settings on washing machines, minimal use of dishwashers and tumble dryers, adopting various strategies when cooking, and avoiding the use of various outdoor appliances.*

- *Step 2. The efficiency of energy use will be improved by changing light bulbs to LEDs, and replacing defunct white goods and other appliances with top of the range (A+ to A+++) appliances, and aiming to switch to gas ovens and hobs when the opportunity arises.*

- *Step 3. Install photovoltaic panels where appropriate.*

- *You can compare your electricity consumption with neighbours and others by accessing sites on the internet.*

CHAPTER 7: HEAT IN THE HOME

The UK has long had a reputation on the continent of Europe for cold and draughty homes. A recent report by the Association for the Conservation of Energy (ACE) studied energy efficiency in the homes of 16 European countries from Iceland and Finland in the north to Slovenia and France further south. The UK was ranked at or within two steps from the bottom for five of six key indicators. It is not for nothing that the report was entitled *The Cold Man of Europe*! In fact the UK's positions in the rankings have mostly got worse between 2011 and 2013. The UK has a long way to go to improve its current housing stock.[220] In 2015 a report on energy efficiency policies among the 28 EU Member States put the UK in the bottom three with Spain and Hungary. The overall ambition and progress of the UK were rated much lower than in a previous survey in 2012 when the UK was ranked 13 out of 28.[221]

The situation in newly built homes is also discouraging. A recent report, which looked in detail at 76 UK homes of varying designs, provided *"strong evidence that carbon emissions from new homes are two or three times higher than design estimates."* The report attributes much of the difference between expected and actual emissions to the behaviour and lack of understanding of the homes' occupants but acknowledges that there are sometimes faults in construction and that some design estimates could be over optimistic.[222] I expect that many readers have come across stories of how brand new homes need attention because the finish or indeed the design was faulty. My plumber has told me that he has worked on new homes built by a local developer which even had leaks in the pipework.

Half of the EU's energy is used for heating and cooling buildings. 75 per cent of this energy comes from fossil fuels, with two thirds of that amount from gas, with the remaining 25 per cent from low-carbon sources.[223] Averaged over the UK, gas accounted for over 43 per cent of the CO_2 emissions from household consumption of energy in 2011.[224] Obviously there will be big variations among households. Because in our own household we are careful to save on electricity the percentage down to gas is a relatively high at 66 per cent. As we saw in Chapter 3, the consumption of gas and other fuels, mostly for heating, accounts for 34 per cent of all emissions by UK households. These figures emphasise that heating is an important source of emissions which should be a prime target for saving energy.

There are many ways to heat a home. They include systems that circulate hot water from a boiler through wall-mounted radiators or underfloor pipes, electrical underfloor heating, circulated warm air, electric radiators, storage heaters, gas and electric fires, wood-burning and oil-burning stoves of various types, and passive solar. Key to reducing the heating demand of all these, except the last three, is some sort of control system to provide heat only when it is needed. It is important to understand these controls since 95 per cent of UK homes now have some form of gas or oil central heating.[225]

So aiming for much more efficient use of energy for heating (and even cooling) in UK homes should be a priority which all better-off home owners can address to some extent.

Suggested actions to save energy and greenhouse gas emissions follow using the three-steps scheme described in Chapter 5.

Step 1. Suggestions for reducing the energy demand of your heating (or cooling) system

Any central heating system, whether fuelled by gas, oil or liquefied petroleum gas (LPG), should have at least a boiler thermostat, a room thermostat that monitors the temperature inside the home and can control the boiler, a programmer or timer (for non-combi boilers), and thermostatic radiator valves (TRVs) on the radiators. A radiator in the same space as the room thermostat should **never** have a TRV fitted. This is because if the TRV senses that it has reached its set point before the room thermostat has reached its own set-point it will switch off the radiator and prevent the room thermostat from ever reaching the temperature to which it has been set (the set point); the boiler will 'hunt' On and Off as it unsuccessfully tries to reach the required temperature.

I now discuss the use of boiler controls as a way of reducing energy demand.

- **The programmer** determines in advance when a central heating boiler is On or Off. The programmer should have separate timers for the heating and hot water operations (if it doesn't it may be relatively simple to exchange the single-channel timer for a dual-channel timer. I did this to our timer some years ago and it took me a matter of minutes to unplug the old timer and plug in the new one to the wall-mounted base plate). For example, the heating timer might be set to switch the boiler On 30 minutes before you get up in the morning and Off 30 minutes or more before you go to bed. If the home is unoccupied during the day the timer can be similarly set to go Off before the last person leaves the home and On before the first person returns (many timers allow for two or three On/Off cycles per day). If the home is occupied all day but is well insulated it should be possible to leave the boiler Off most of the day anyway. The exact On and Off times will depend on the season (see next bullet point) and how quickly the home heats up and cools down. Every home will be different and you will need to experiment to find what timer settings suit you and your home. The heating timer should definitely **not** normally leave the boiler in a permanently On state because the temperature can be allowed to drop at night when the occupants are in bed as well as when the home is unoccupied. The hot water

110

timer settings will depend on demand i.e. when, and how much, hot water is required. If you have a well insulated, hot-water storage tank it may be sufficient for the boiler to heat water just once a day.

• There is normally no need for the central heating system in an insulated home to run in the summer months. Therefore it is worth considering what should happen in the intermediate **spring and autumn** seasons. Ideally as cooler days, and nights, approach one should delay getting into the regular winter timetable of the boiler timer as long as possible. One could set up the timer to run the boiler for shorter periods, or not at all, and just switch it on when the home gets too cool. Or maybe, because the home still warms up naturally during the day, one could run the boiler only in the evenings. Alternatively, if the home has another, lower-carbon source of heat such as a wood-burning stove, that could be used in cool evenings. Clearly the reverse situation applies as spring approaches with warmer days.

• The next most important control is the **room thermostat**. This is usually wall mounted with a circular adjustable control marked in degrees Celsius or with a digital display. This thermostat will switch the boiler On or Off according to the set point. Of course while the programmer/timer has the boiler in an Off state the room thermostat will have no effect. You will often read about turning this thermostat down by one degree or more to save energy and this can be very effective. A temperature range of 18 to 21°C is usually recommended for living areas. It appears to be politically incorrect, or at least is seldom seen, to suggest that as people turn down the room thermostat they should wear warmer clothes but in fact this is a very sensible and obvious way to keep warm. It is certainly cheaper to wear a sleeveless body warmer in cold weather, and even some thermal underwear, than to pay for higher energy bills.

- **The boiler thermostat** determines the temperature at which hot water leaves the boiler before it carries heat around the home. This is another of those unhelpful rotary knobs with just numbers or even a curved wedge-shaped symbol without accurate temperatures. If the radiators get too hot to the touch and possibly create a danger to the occupants then turn down this knob but normally it should be at least in a middle position. The hotter the setting of the boiler thermostat the quicker the home will warm up.

- **Thermostatic radiator valves** (TRVs) can be used to set different radiators (and rooms) to different temperatures. For example, a room that is rarely used can have a low setting, bedrooms could be slightly warmer and living areas could be warmer still. Some TRVs are programmable in that they can be set to different temperatures at different times of day. The TRV will turn the radiator off as the air around it reaches the set point and On again as the air cools below the set point. Again, TRVs have uncalibrated numbers on a scale from 1 to 6, for example, and experimentation is required to find the required setting.

- Some heating control systems are even more sophisticated than I have described. It is possible to install **programmable room thermostats** that allow for different temperatures at different times of day. You can even arrange for different zones in your home to have different time and temperature settings. It is also possible to control your heating system remotely via a computer, tablet or smart phone if you want the heating to come on earlier or later than programmed. It is not evident that these extra degrees of control will necessarily save a lot of energy but they will help.

All the above remarks emphasise how important it is to make an effort to understand all your heating controls. A few minutes spent refreshing your memory and perhaps experimenting with different settings is well worthwhile. There is some truth in the statement by the UK government in a report in 2013 that *"Central heating system controls seem to live incognito in many homes. Many people may not recognise or understand their central heating control system."*[225]

For the five per cent of homes without some form of oil or gas central heating there are limited options mostly dependent on electricity. While electricity may indeed be the heating source of the future, as many countries come to depend more on renewable energy and less on fossil fuels to generate electricity, it is currently less environmentally friendly than gas. An exception is the use of electricity in a heat pump, which can be described as a form of renewable heating, which is described in Step 3 later in the chapter.

- **Electric radiators** are usually slimmer than water-filled radiators. They may be wall mounted or free standing. They have the advantage that they generate heat rapidly after being switched on. Electric radiators can include a thermostat and can be controlled by a programmer, either centrally or individually, or manually (even using a remote control).

- **Storage heaters** are heated by electricity, usually in the 'off-peak' night hours when electricity is cheaper (and CO_2 emissions per kWh tend to be less; see Chapter 4 for a detailed discussion). A storage heater, as the name implies, stores heat in special bricks. Modern heaters are better insulated and have an internal thermostat that controls the temperature reached by the bricks (the input setting). An output setting determines the room temperature (provided some stored heat remains). A fan can also be used to boost heat output. A system with a Celect-type controller will monitor heaters in all rooms and automatically control how much heat is stored or released in different rooms.[226]

- Finally, the **heating of hot water** will normally, unless you have a combi boiler, be controlled by the boiler's programmable timer and a special thermostat which is usually to be found about

113

two-thirds of the way up on the outside of the hot-water cylinder. This thermostat prevents the water overheating. Set the timer to match the times of hot water demand in your home such as for showers and washing the dishes. Assuming your cylinder is both well insulated, so the water should keep hot for at least twenty-four hours, and large enough to match the demand, then a single boost from the boiler once a day should be enough. The cylinder thermostat will ensure that the water does not become dangerously hot. Choose a setting of 60 to 65°C to kill bacteria that can cause Legionnaire's disease. If the boiler thermostat is set to a lower temperature then the cylinder thermostat will never reach its set point! Some homes still have electrical immersion heaters fitted within their hot water cylinders. The presence of an immersion heater can be recognised by the electrical cable fitted to the top of the cylinder; they are usually switched On and Off by a nearby wall switch. Immersion heaters are best left unused if you have a gas boiler because, as already mentioned, electricity is a more polluting fuel than gas. See Step 3 of this chapter for heating water with a solar panel or Chapter 6 for using surplus PV electricity for heating water with an immersion heater. If you have a combi boiler the hot water temperature will be set by the boiler thermostat.

• Most hot water is used for **personal washing and bathing**. It makes a huge difference to your consumption of hot water whether you take a shower, a power shower or a bath and for how long and how often you do so. For example, a 4-minute shower might consume six litres of hot water, a 4-minute power shower 30 litres and a bath a massive 150 litres (twenty-five times more than a simple shower). Some showers can be fitted with a special head that mixes air with the water and uses even less hot water. Whatever your type of shower you can also save energy by switching off the water while soaping yourself down. It might help to remember that heating ten litres of water in a gas boiler consumes around 0.64 kWh of energy or causes the emissions of 0.12 kg of CO_2.[227] The choice is yours but you can see how taking fewer baths, taking 4-minute showers and avoiding power showers altogether can soon cut your demand for hot water and the associated carbon emissions while allowing you to keep clean. On the other hand, if your hot water is provided solely by a solar panel it will have caused almost zero emissions and you can enjoy a shower, or even a bath, with a clear conscience.

• In most homes today efficient **cooling** is probably less of a problem than heating but, as the summers get hotter due to global warming, more and more of us will start to find we want to keep cool indoors. It is easy to take this to extremes and I suspect we have all been in a situation where we had to put on a sweater because the temperature of the air conditioning in an office or public building was set too low. I have a friend whose father prides himself on saving energy by keeping his home cool in winter but unfortunately he adopts the same strategy by using air-conditioning in the summer. As discussed in the next section, insulation is key to keeping cool. Just as insulation keeps a home warm in winter so it will keep it cool in summer. So here are some strategies for keeping cool. The first thing to recognise is that the source of unwelcome heat, which is the Sun, changes its direction and height during the day. Windows let in a wide range of solar radiation, particularly in summer when the Sun is low during the early morning and late afternoon, and yet the window glass tends to trap some of the returning long-wavelength infrared radiation in the room so the room heats up. This is why it is sensible to draw curtains and/or blinds on the sunny side of the home or even to install external shutters (which are very popular and practical in southern Europe). Draughts help us to keep cool because of the heat lost when dampness on the skin evaporates. Draughts can be induced, if the home is occupied, by opening windows or doors on opposite sides of the home. Finally taking a cool shower or simply wiping the body with a wet cloth can help one to cool down. If a home is unoccupied during the day draw all the curtains and blinds, especially on the east- and west-facing windows.

Step 2. Suggestions for using your heating (and cooling) system more efficiently

Using the heating system more efficiently really means keeping the heat in the home for longer, which comes down to insulation, and having a more efficient central heating boiler. Heat is lost from a home wherever the outer surface of a wall, window, outside door, roof (or ceiling) or floor is cooler than the interior. More heat is lost the greater the temperature difference between the inside and the outside. Heat is also lost through draughts in ill-fitting windows, doors and other gaps such as around pipes passing through outside walls and chimneys. There is no avoiding the fact that, especially in winter, it is often colder outside than in and so it is worth taking the trouble to minimise heat loss. Some moderate costs may be involved but this is where a better-off home owner will have the resources to tackle the problem. More detailed information than is provided here can be obtained from the Energy Saving Trust which can provide expert advice on home insulation.[228]

Insulation works on air! This may seem a strange statement but air is a good insulator and the secret of most insulation is the way that it uses air trapped in tiny spaces in the insulating material to prevent heat loss. Therefore many insulating materials are like solid foams or fibrous quilts; the thicker the material, the more heat is retained and for longer. Air gaps, such as between the two halves of a cavity wall, offer some insulation but heat can be carried across the gap by movements of the air driven by the difference in temperature between the two sides. You may need expert help to calculate and choose the best type of insulation for your particular situation.

• Probably the most heat, up to a third, is lost through the **outside walls** of an uninsulated home. Walls can be either solid walls (mostly in homes built before 1919) or cavity walls (in homes built mostly, but not entirely, after the 1920s). **Cavity walls** are thicker because there is a void space between the inner and outer leaf. They can be recognised by the pattern in the bricks on the outside; the bricks are laid so that you see only the longer side. **A solid wall** is usually thinner (if built with bricks; an old stone house for example can have very thick walls). If the thickness of a brick wall at a window or door is 260 mm or less the wall will not have a cavity. In a solid wall the bricks in any one layer are usually laid alternately showing the longer side and the end side along the layer. This characteristic pattern has variants but if you see that lots of bricks were laid end on to the wall then you are probably looking at a solid wall. In homes built since the 1990s sheets of insulation material should have been placed in the cavity as the wall was built. Insulating a wall with an unfilled cavity is relatively cheap and can be very effective (almost three-quarters of homes with cavity walls in Great Britain have already been treated in this way).[229] Holes are drilled in the mortar of the outer wall and some sort of foam, fibre or beads is pumped in to fill the void space. The process is quick (one day or less) and the insulating effect is felt immediately. Take professional advice if you have a damp problem or your wall is very exposed to rain. Insulation can be added to the inside or the outside of a solid outside wall (only one in 20 of homes in Great Britain with solid walls have been insulated this way). Insulating the inside involves fixing insulated panels to the inner wall. The panels consist of plasterboard with an insulating layer attached. This is more disruptive, some services such as radiators and electrical sockets may have to be moved, and it also means that the room will effectively become smaller (by around 40 mm on each outside wall). Obviously adding insulation to the outside wall may change its appearance and

117

there may be planning restrictions (see Chapter 9). External insulating panels are thinner but will require some rendering or dry cladding to be applied over them. I shall describe an example of a 'SuperHome' that adopted this approach to a cavity wall in Chapter 9.

• **Windows** lose heat not only through the glass but also through the window frame itself; the amount of heat lost depends on the material – whether wood, aluminium, steel or unplasticised polyvinyl chloride (uPVC). Heat may also be lost through draughts in ill-fitting frames and opening windows. Some of this heat loss can be avoided, even if the window is single glazed, by installing thick curtains and/or blinds which are regularly drawn at dusk. Another option is to use secondary glazing. Secondary glazing usually involves adding a pane of glass or plastic sheeting on an extra frame placed close up against the existing window frame but this is never as effective as double-glazing. External shutters, although rarely seen in the UK because they require windows that open inwards, can help as well. From the insulation point of view it is certainly well worth replacing single-glazed windows with double- or even triple-glazed windows. You will also gain extra sound proofing. The British Fenestration Rating Council (BFRC) provides a rating scheme that shows how well different designs of window perform using a scale of A+ (best) to E (worst). The rating takes account of heat loss through the glass and frame as well as air leakage through the window's seals. It balances heat losses against solar energy gains. Because new windows should last for around 20 years it is worth paying for the best rating that you can afford. Modern double glazing has a wider gap between the two panes than earlier versions. The gap may even contain unusual gases, such as argon, xenon or krypton, which conduct heat less efficiently across the gap than air or even a near vacuum which will conduct almost no heat. One final aspect is the use of low-emissivity (low-e) glass. This means that one of the inner glass surfaces is coated with an invisible layer of metal-oxide which lets in ultraviolet radiation from the Sun but inhibits the passage of returning infrared radiation from the room (it acts a bit like a greenhouse gas in the atmosphere).

- **External doors** are fortunately less numerous in a home than windows but they can waste heat too. The insulation properties of external doors are often described by their U-value; lower U-values indicate better insulation. We used to have a single-glazed front door, with a large slot and flap for letters, which also leaked air around the edges. Once we replaced it with a modern double-glazed door designed for low heat conductivity, and with no slot for the post (I installed a metal letter box on the wall outside instead), the hall immediately became warmer. Since our central heating room thermostat is located in the hall this had a knock-on effect on our boiler usage and on saving energy. For various reasons we did not replace the frame of the front door at the same time but when we replaced the back door we bought a factory made, matching pair of frame and double-glazed door. Consequently, we got rid of all draughts there as well. I think that the above experience tells you what needs to be done if you think you are losing heat through any of your outside doors.

- **Loft insulation** is probably the most familiar type of insulation to many home owners because it can be carried out by any competent DIYer (70 per cent of homes in Great Britain already have at least 125mm of loft insulation). Typically, some form of fibrous insulation material (often fibre glass) is laid down between and over the joists that support the ceiling below (but never under water tanks if present). Although 270 mm of insulation is recommended rolls of insulation material are sold in rolls of varying and lesser thickness with widths that fit standard joist separations. The trick is to choose rolls whose width matches your joist separation and also fits the depth of the joists. If your joists have non-standard separations the insulation can be cut to size relatively easily with a knife or garden shears. A second set of rolls can then be laid across the first at right angles to cover the joists and to make up the thickness to around 270 mm. This type of insulation lasts a long time but is easily disturbed and degraded by stepping between the joists. Compressing the insulation under a boarded walkway or even a heavy box will also cause almost half of the insulating properties to be lost.[230] An alternative solution is to use solid foam insulation under walkways instead; this will provide twice as much insulation as glass fibre in the same space. Finally care has to be taken near the eaves to ensure that ventilation of the loft space is not blocked by the insulation material. Applying insulation in this way means that the loft, and any stored contents, will experience the extremes of the outside weather. In fact, in summer the roof is likely to trap heat and it can become very warm indeed.

- Alternatively loft insulation can be applied under a **pitched roof**. This is the way forward if you want to use the loft space as an extra room all year round. Insulation can be applied as solid panels, snugly fitting the space between the rafters, which are then covered by insulating plaster-board. If there are also hard-to-reach void spaces, for example around a dormer window installed as part of a roof extension, it is possible to blow insulation material into the void. You will need expert help to do this.

- Insulating **flat roofs** is possible but requires specialist intervention and is only recommended when the roof has to be replaced or renewed for some other reason.

- After walls and roofs, **floors at ground level** are probably the next biggest cause of heat loss from a home. Modern houses tend to have solid concrete floors and it is potentially very disruptive to try and improve on their insulation. Either the floor has to be dug up and re-laid or a layer of insulation has to be added which raises the floor level by at least 25 mm. Older homes often have floorboards laid across joists which are 'suspended' over a void space which is usually ventilated by means of air bricks inserted in the external walls surrounding the space. If the void space can be accessed, and is big enough to work in, then snug fitting, solid foam insulation panels or batts can be fixed in between the floor joists from below. Alternatively, the floor boards can be lifted and the insulation material inserted from above between the joists before the boards are replaced. In either case any gaps between the floor and skirting boards around the edges of the room must be filled with sealant in order to avoid draughts; gaps between boards should also be filled for the same reason. The floors of upper storey rooms that lie over a cold space can be similarly insulated.

- Next we should consider **getting rid of draughts**. Gaps in all external walls, for instance where a pipe passes through a wall and around window frames, and between floorboards and around skirting boards can be filled with a proprietary flexible filler. Draughts around doors and opening windows can be reduced by applying special draught-excluding strips; you will need to choose the product that best suits your situation. Loft hatches are another source of draughts and even the hatch cover itself is worth insulating with a layer of solid foam. I advertised on a local web site saying I needed a small piece of foam insulation - it would have been wasteful to buy a whole 1.2m by 2.4m sheet – and found someone who had just finished a job and was about to take an offcut of about the right size to the local dump.

- If you have successfully excluded most draughts you might reasonably be concerned about where the air you need to breathe will come from! Adequate **ventilation** is also important to reduce steam and the growth of mould on cold walls. Extraction fans in bathrooms and kitchens can help. More sophisticated designs of the most 'air tight' new homes include mechanical heat-recovery ventilation systems. These use fans that recover heat, from the extracted air, which is used to pre-heat incoming fresh air. On the other hand simply opening windows wide for as long as it takes to change the air will remove damp air without noticeably cooling the walls. I calculated what happens if the air in my bathroom cools by ten degrees if I open the window. It turns out that the heat taken from the walls and ceiling, after closing the window, to gradually warm up the air again, will only cool the surrounding plasterboard and plaster on the walls and ceiling by three quarters of a degree. This happens because air is much less dense than brick so it holds much less heat.

• If your gas boiler is more than about 15 years old possibly the most effective way to use the heating system more efficiently is to **replace the boiler**. In recent years gas boilers have become up to 89 per cent efficient meaning that 89 per cent of the heat generated is used to produce hot water. Modern boilers are designed to recycle the heat that previously was lost in gases going up the flue. Waste heat is extracted by condensing some of the flue gases which are then used to pre-heat the cold water entering the boiler. Hence such boilers are known as **condensing boilers**. If you replace a boiler more than 15 years old, which may be only 65-70 per cent efficient, your new boiler should provide 37-27 per cent more heat than the old one. By law, since 2005, all new and replacement boilers have to be condensing boilers anyway.

• Many older central heating systems store hot water in a cylinder tank which is topped up from a cold water tank, usually in the loft, as hot water is used up. When you replace your boiler you may also have the option of installing a **combi boiler** so named because it performs the combined functions of supplying central heating and hot water. It does this on demand. In other words it doesn't require a hot water cylinder or a cold water tank in the loft to top it up. If you turn on a hot tap the combi boiler produces hot water almost instantaneously. Combi boilers suit smaller homes. Where it is likely that more than one hot water tap will be used at a time the flow rate from each tap may be insufficient because combi boilers are designed to provide hot water up to a certain maximum rate.

- While considering the storage of hot water in a **cylinder tank** it is worth reviewing the insulation of the cylinder. It is clearly wasteful to heat water that is then stored in a cylinder that leaks heat, however much you like to have a warm airing cupboard. Modern cylinders come already clad in factory-applied solid-foam insulation but if the outside of the tank still feels warm why not add a cheap hot-water cylinder insulating jacket around the outside? When I did this to my own cylinder the water temperature remained two degrees higher after 12 hours.

- Finally we come to **air conditioning**. A well insulated home should stay cooler in summer as well as warmer in winter. But if a home is exposed to direct sunshine for an appreciable part of the day it may overheat and this is likely to become more of a problem as summer temperatures rise due to global warming. Simple strategies to prevent a home overheating were described in Step 1. The immediate technical solution does not have to be the installation of air conditioning units. External blinds or brise soleil (French for literally 'break sun'), a fixed set of vertical slats to create shade, can be sited on east and west facing windows which experience low sun in the early morning and late afternoon (the midday sun is almost overhead and causes less heating through the windows). Alternatively you can install solar control glass. This allows sunlight to pass through a window or façade while radiating and reflecting away a large proportion of the Sun's heat. The indoor space stays bright and much cooler than would be the case if normal glass were used. If you feel that air conditioning is unavoidable consider using an absorption air conditioner, a form of air-air heat pump, driven by heat from gas or solar hot water, which will cause fewer emissions, unless you can access renewable electricity, rather than an electric air conditioner.

Step 3. Generating your own heat

Just as you can generate your own electricity using renewable energy from the Sun so you can produce renewable heat in the form of warm water or air.

• Hot water can be generated by a **solar thermal panel**. One or two panels, each about two square metres in area, will be enough for most homes. Solar thermal panels ideally should be placed in a south facing location to catch direct sunlight. The panels have special dark surfaces that absorb direct solar radiation and heat up water that is circulated through the panel. In essence the system is very simple and consists of the panel(s), a well insulated, hot-water storage tank and a pump and pipework that circulates the water (or more often an antifreeze solution) whenever the panel temperature exceeds the tank temperature by a pre-set amount. The circulated water is in a closed pressurised system that includes a coil-shaped heat exchanger in the tank. A solar thermal panel may provide all your hot water in mid-summer but at other times, even on cold but sunny days in winter, it pre-heats water that will be brought up to the required temperature later by your boiler. The antifreeze protects the pipework in winter. Should the outside temperature ever fall below a pre-set panel temperature the pump can be used to circulate warm water from the tank into the panel to prevent freezing. The system is optimised by adjusting the flow rate; too fast and not enough heat is extracted in the heat exchanger coil and too slow and the panel will get excessively hot. The only moving part in the system is the pump which tends to have a shorter lifetime than the panel but is normally simple to replace.

• I now describe **heat pumps**. A fridge takes heat from its contents (food and drink) and delivers this heat to the fridge's surroundings by a heat exchanger coil usually situated on the back of the fridge (if you've never tested this take a moment to put your hand over the coil and be surprised at how warm it is). A heat pump is often described as a refrigerator that works backwards. Put more crudely, if you imagine, as a thought experiment, the fridge inserted snugly and facing outwards in a hole in an outside wall with its door wide open then you would have a (very crude) system that would take heat from the outside and warm the inside of the building. In essence this is how a heat pump works; it absorbs heat from the air, or even from a body of water or the ground, and uses it to produce warm water or air for indoor heating purposes.

Some purists do not consider heat pumps to be a source of renewable energy because, although the primary source of heat is indirect energy from the Sun, heat pumps cannot work without the use of electricity by the pump which may not necessarily have come from a renewable source. On the other hand I would argue that heat pumps are a means of extracting solar energy for heating in a way that is often about three to four times more efficient than directly using the electricity itself to produce the heat. The amount of this super-efficiency, called the Coefficient of Performance (COP), is important because remember that natural gas produces around 2.7 times less emissions than electricity when delivering the same amount of heat energy. So if the average COP of a heat pump throughout the year is not more than 2.7 then a better option would be to use mains gas for heating, provided it is available. This is why heat pumps are most suitable for homes that cannot access a mains gas supply. But there is also an argument that the carbon intensity of electricity (the amount of CO_2 produced per kilowatt.hour) will decrease with time as fossil fuels are phased out, so all new houses, even if they can access gas, should in the long term plan to use electricity for heating instead of natural gas. This is especially true if the house is being, or can eventually be, fitted with PV panels. Even so, installing a heat pump in an existing off-gas home can be very disruptive because new underfloor heating pipes or larger radiators or air ducts, depending on the type of arrangement, will have to be installed. For all these reasons a heat pump is best installed in a new home as it is being built.

The temperature of the air or water output from a heat pump rarely exceeds 45°C. Heat pumps work more efficiently the smaller the difference in temperature between the heat source and the output water or air. To maximise the COP it is very important to understand and optimise the controls in the system. The COP depends very much on the installation and prevailing conditions.

•   **An air source heat pump** blows outside air over a heat exchanger that allows the cooler refrigerant to absorb heat. This refrigerant is then compressed and pumped through the device in the normal way. The extracted heat can be used to produce warm water or warm air. Air source heat pumps should work at air temperatures well below freezing but they can become blocked by ice in cold and damp conditions. An advantage of an air source heat pump is that, unlike a ground source heat pump, it does not require a large area of land in which to bury hoses.

•   **A ground-source heat pump** extracts heat from the ground. It does not use geothermal energy as such, that is energy derived from the radioactive decay of certain elements in the Earth's crust and deeper layers, but energy that comes from the Sun which heats up the ground on a seasonal basis. Heat is extracted from hoses buried in trenches at a depth of around two metres, where the temperature is about 10°C all year round. Around 50 m^2 of ground area is required for every kW of output depending on ground conditions.[231] If space is not available then one or more deep (100m or more) boreholes can be used instead. Alternatively, one company has come up with the idea of combining solar thermal panels to heat the ground under the home in summer and a matrix of shallow 1.5m boreholes to extract the heat when needed.[232]

• Other heat pump arrangements can extract heat from any large body of water or even a river subject to regulations on the allowable fall in temperature of the water that is returned to the body of water or river after heat has been extracted from it.

Further information about heat pumps can be obtained from the Energy Saving Trust at http://www.energysavingtrust.org.uk/domestic/renewable-heat.

How are you doing with reducing gas consumption?

It may encourage you to compare your gas consumption with other homes in your postcode area and local authority area and, nationally, with similar-sized homes.

You can compare your annual gas consumption with other domestic users in your complete postcode area as follows. Download the relevant Excel spreadsheet for 2013 from www.gov.uk/government/statistics/postcode-level-gas-estimates-2013-experimental. DECC describe the data as experimental apparently because the methodology used to produce them is still under development. The data appear to have been corrected for variations in outside temperature. Use Find & Select > Find > Find Next to locate the entry for your postcode. Columns D and E give the mean (average) and median consumptions for your postcode. By definition there are as many homes with consumptions greater than the median value as less than it. If everyone was able to reduce their consumption to be less than the median in 2013 then overall consumption would decrease dramatically! The average annual gas consumption in different local authority areas is available at www.gov.uk/government/statistical-data-sets/gas-sales-and-numbers-of-customers-by-region-and-local-authority.

How are you doing with reducing gas consumption? (continued)

Download the file called 'Gas sales and numbers of customers by region and local authority: 2005 to 2014' as an Excel spreadsheet. Click on the '2014r' tab at the bottom of the spreadsheet. Use Find & Select > Find > Find Next to locate the entry for your local authority. Columns M and N give mean (average) and median consumptions of domestic gas.

To help you compare your consumption with similarly sized homes the following table gives median annual gas consumptions for differently sized homes in England in 2011.

Home	Median annual gas consumption (kWh/year)
Terraced house – mid-terrace	12,900
Terraced house – end-terrace	13,400
Semi-detached house	15,500
Detached house	19,500
Bungalow	13,100
Flat	8,800

Data from Table 2 in Hulme, Jack, Beaumont, Adele, and Summers, Claire. "Report 3: Metered Fuel Consumption: Including Annex on High Energy Users." BRE/DECC, December 2013. Table 2 also provides data on median consumption by dwelling age and floor area. Fig.5 of this publication indicates median gas consumptions by floor area.

Summary

- *Heating (and cooling) homes should be a prime target for saving energy.*
- *Step 1. To reduce the energy demand for heating it is essential to understand the controls of the heating system, whether a boiler or a storage heater. These include the programmer/timer, the room thermostat, the boiler thermostat and thermostatic radiator valves (TRVs). There are also simple strategies for minimising hot water demand such as taking a shower instead of a bath, replacing the showerhead with one that entrains air and turning off the water while you apply soap or shampoo.*
- *Step 2. To use the heating system more efficiently it is essential to have a condensing boiler and a well insulated home. Insulation includes treating cavity walls or outside solid walls and installing suitable double glazing, external doors, loft insulation, floors (where practical) and excluding draughts. Insulation will also keep the home cool in summer.*
- *Step 3. Low-carbon renewable heat can be generated from solar hot-water panels and heat pumps.*
- *You can compare your gas consumption with neighbours and others by accessing sites on the internet.*

CHAPTER 8: FREQUENT TRIPS AND NON-BUSINESS TRAVEL

Now we come to the third and final set of emissions that are relatively easy to estimate. These are the emissions from getting about in our daily lives, mostly in the repetitive trips that are made almost on a daily basis to commute to and from work, take children to and from school and buy food. But in addition there are those other, non-business journeys, usually further afield, that we make to visit family and friends or to go on holiday. As we saw in Chapter 3, the use of private cars, public transport and international non-business flights account for a very substantial 42 per cent of UK household emissions. The results of a survey in Oxfordshire, also mentioned in Chapter 3, showed that this is potentially an area in which the better off can make a substantial contribution to reducing emissions.[233]

The UK government's Department for Transport conducts regular National Travel Surveys in England. The latest survey in 2014 reveals some interesting statistics about how far and how often we make certain types of trip.[234] We need to remember that the reported figures are averages and there may be large variations between the different classifications of 'trippers' that the survey covers.[235]

Suggested actions to save energy and greenhouse gas emissions follow using the three-steps scheme described in Chapter 5. I propose separate sets of actions for Frequent trips, and Non-business travel and holidays abroad.

Frequent trips

38 per cent of all trips are made for shopping, personal business and transporting children (excluding taking them to school), 30 per cent for visiting friends or other leisure activities,

16 per cent for commuting, 12 per cent for education (including taking children to school) and, surprisingly, only three per cent of trips are for business travel.

To get a feel for which trips contribute most to UK households', or rather English households', carbon footprint we need to consider the distances travelled and, eventually, the modes of transport. The survey shows that for distances travelled the rankings are somewhat different. 39 per cent of the distances travelled are taken up with visiting friends or other leisure activities, 25 per cent with shopping, personal business and transporting children, 20 per cent with commuting, ten per cent for business and only five per cent for education (including taking children to school). Ignoring business travel, which is beyond the scope of this book, it is clear that the trips that on average are longest, by a factor of two or more, are those for leisure activities, visiting friends and commuting. However, the definition of 'other leisure activities' includes not only trips to places of entertainment and sport and day trips but also holidays which I shall consider separately in the next section.

By far the largest number of trips overall (64 per cent) are made by car, either as a driver or passenger, followed by 22 per cent of trips made on foot. Astonishingly almost half (49 per cent) of trips under two miles are made by car, as are around 80 per cent of all longer trips. Only ten per cent of trips and 15 per cent of the distances are covered by public transport.

Finally, we should note some typical emissions from public transport. Obviously the emissions per passenger for all forms of public transport will depend on the proportion of seats that are occupied; this is known as the load factor. In England in 2016 the emissions from buses (outside London), national rail trains and coaches, assuming appropriate average load factors, are estimated by DECC to be 120, 49 and 29 grams per passenger.kilometre respectively.[236,237] These are all considerably less than the 180 grams per kilometre of the average UK car (see later) unless the car carries at least one passenger. As a general rule the modes of land transport with the least emissions are walking and cycling, followed by bus and car for shorter distances, and coach followed by train and car for longer distances (see table).

The commute to work is something over which we have control in the sense that we can, to a greater or lesser extent, choose where we work and where we live. In reality it is not always that simple because of the cost of housing, the possibly specialised nature of our work and opportunities for employment, and also because of the options available for the mode of travel whether it be by car, train or other public transport. There has been a fall in the number of commuting trips since the mid-1990s, perhaps as working from home has become more common and practical. Car trips for commuting have the lowest occupancy rates (1.2 occupants) of all such trips.

Typical emissions figures for various modes of land transport

Mode of transport	Emissions (g CO_2e) per passenger.kilometre
Private car (driver only)	180 (average figure only)
Bus (outside London)	120 (assuming load factor)
Private car (one pass.)	90 (average figure only)
Train	49 (assuming load factor)
Coach	29 (assuming load factor)
Cycling	0 (excluding manufacture and maintenance of bicycle, and any extra food energy consumed)
Walking	0 (excluding wear and tear of footwear, and any extra food energy consumed)

Over the years the National Travel Surveys in England have shown some interesting trends. Since the mid-1990s the share of walking and cycling has decreased from 28 per cent to 24 per cent of all trips and trips on foot have declined by 30 per cent. The proportion of trips by car and public transport has increased slightly. But looking outside London, which accounts for much of the increase in trips by public transport, the number of trips by bus fell by 20 per cent since the mid-1990s. These are good signs in that the number of trips and the average trip distances have fallen but the distance travelled by car while commuting has barely changed.

Finally, and very relevant to the topic of this book, people in the highest 20 per cent of household income groups are shown to travel more than twice as far as people in the lowest 20 per cent income group. The highest 20 per cent income group travel mostly by car, but by other means too, whereas almost a quarter of the lowest 20 per cent income group do not have access to a car. Highest income households make about three times as many trips for commuting or business as do the lowest income households.

So what can we conclude from this array of data from the travel surveys about the daily trips we make? The main points are:

- Almost two-thirds of the distance travelled is for visiting friends, other leisure activities (including holidays), shopping, transporting children and personal business.
- Almost half of all trips under two miles are made by car.
- Commuting cars carry very few passengers.
- Home working is increasing.
- The use of buses outside London has decreased substantially since the mid-1990s.
- Walking has declined.
- Higher income households make more commuting/business trips and travel further than lower income households.

So here, on the basis of these conclusions, are some suggestions for cutting the emissions from daily or other frequent trips.

Step 1. Suggestions for reducing the emissions involved in frequent trips

It is easy to get into fixed habits when we make our daily or frequent trips. To reduce emissions from these sources it is a good idea to step back and review our habits.

- For a fit person **walking and cycling** (if you already own a bike), instead of driving, are both ways to reduce emissions from trips of under two miles at zero cost. Walking up to two miles takes up to 40 minutes and cycling two miles will take about ten minutes. Given that a parking space has to be found for a car it may in fact be quickest to cycle. Either walking or cycling will provide healthy exercise and help to meet the recommendation for adults of working age of at least 150 minutes of moderate aerobic activity every week.[238] Although your journey might take a bit longer you won't have to fit in an exercise session at another time. You'll kill two birds with one stone as the saying goes.

- **Plan car trips** so as to carry out more than one errand at a time. This can save at least one trip whether visiting friends, conducting other leisure activities, shopping, transporting children and carrying out personal business and also save time.

- **Discard one car.** In households with more than one car it is worth reviewing the need for having two (or more) cars. The National Travel Survey in 2014 showed that at least 45 per cent of households in the top 40 per cent of income groups have two or more cars and around five per cent of households have three or more cars.[234] However, having fewer cars in a household will reduce emissions only if the total distance driven by all cars declines but this may encourage the adoption of some of the other suggestions made here for getting around without a car.

- There are often ways to save on emissions from **commuting** whether it means walking or cycling to the station, sharing a lift by car or even taking a bus instead of driving. If you don't know anyone at work with whom to share your commute by car there are free schemes such as Liftshare to arrange lifts online.[239] Information on how this and other schemes work can be found at www.which.co.uk/cars/driving/car-hire-and-car-clubs/car-share-schemes/. Changing how you travel to work, even for one day a week, can potentially reduce your footprint. If time is short in the mornings try taking a possibly slower but less polluting way home after work. Another approach, if you can work flexible hours, is to get to work early and to come home early. A friend of mine does this because the roads are much less congested outside the morning and evening rush hours, thereby ensuring fewer emissions from driving, and he has time to spend with his two young children too when he gets home from work in the late afternoon.

- **Home working**, even once a week or a fortnight, is worth trying too and can reduce your footprint from commuting by at least 10 per cent. With modern communications you will not be out of touch with the office and in fact there is plenty of evidence to suggest that you may work more productively at home with fewer distractions. You will also gain time and save on the cost of the commute, if you live well away from your work, but the downside may be that you have to acquire some office equipment and in winter you have to pay for heating your home.

Step 2. Suggestions for carrying out frequent trips more efficiently

- An extreme, but entirely rational, choice is to **get rid of the car** altogether! The rationale for this is that from a general point of view a car is a really poor use of resources. What other item costs so much yet stands idle for a huge percentage, maybe well over 90 per cent, of the time? Most cars have at least four seats which rarely are all occupied. The overall weight of a car exceeds the minimal payload, meaning the weight of the driver, by around 15 times. So it could make a lot of sense to ditch your car and join a car club scheme such as the 'enterprise car club'.[240] Such schemes work best in cities where much of the time one can rely on public transport anyway. In effect you hire a car by the hour using a smart phone with the minimum of bureaucracy. Alternatively you could use a taxi, depending on the type of journey that you are planning. A car club car and a taxi are good examples of well used resources. For longer periods of time you could hire a car by the day in the normal way.

• If you use a car for many trips one simple way to do this more efficiently, other than carrying out more than one errand at a time, is to **change the car** for a model that emits less CO_2. But try to ensure that you get hold of, or can estimate, emissions figures that include real world driving when making comparisons and before making the change (see Chapter 4). Perhaps the first aspect to review is whether you should choose a car with a manual or an automatic gearbox. I was surprised to read on Parkers well known car buying web site that *"Now, with electronics monitoring the car's efficiency and with more gears on hand, automatics are frequently more economical than the manual versions. With greater fuel efficiency comes lower CO_2 emissions too."*[241] Automatic gearboxes in higher mpg cars are about two per cent more efficient. Changing a car also offers an opportunity to consider the relative benefits of petrol, diesel, hybrid and all-electric models. From the carbon footprint point of view diesel cars always outperform petrol models but they emit more particulates and have higher emissions of nitrogen oxides, which are bad for health, and so are less suitable for heavy urban driving. The total emissions from electric (and some hybrid) cars will depend on whether the electricity used to charge the car

137

battery comes from a low-carbon source, such as a supplier who provides 100 per cent renewable electricity, or a coal, gas or nuclear power station (manufacturers claim that the exhaust pipe emissions are zero, which is correct, but this ignores the emissions at the power station). If a hybrid car gets its electricity from a petrol or diesel engine then it still burns a fossil fuel and emits CO_2 but it gains in efficiency from features such as regenerative braking and tends to have 15-30 per cent less CO_2 emissions per kilometre that a conventional car.[242] Lastly, as we have seen, the manufacture of a car involves embodied emissions. So when replacing a car that has come to the end of its useful life the better solution, from the personal emissions point of view, is to buy a second-hand car rather than a brand new one. The critical decision is deciding when a car is reaching the end of its useful life. Ideally, if the lives of cars could be safely prolonged, then fewer new cars would need to be built thereby reducing emissions.

• **Avoid short car journeys** because it can take any non-electric car up to five miles before the engine has warmed up enough to run at maximum efficiency so it will be using extra fuel and causing even more emissions in the first five miles. Also catalytic converters, which reduce emissions of NOx, carbon monoxide and volatile organic compounds, but not CO_2, only operate correctly once the engine has fully warmed up.

• Another approach would be to **buy a bicycle** or, if you live in a particularly hilly area or are concerned about your fitness, you could buy an electric bike. Panniers can be used to carry shopping and other items. Very young children can be carried on a variety of special front or rear child bike seats but there are also many other options for older children including trailers, tagalongs and even box bikes.[243]

- The time taken over, and emissions from, any trip by car will depend on the route taken and **traffic congestion**. If possible, plan the time of day of your trip to avoid congestion.

- **Practise eco-driving**. You can reduce emissions from your car by at least ten per cent simply by driving it in an energy efficient manner. This is called eco-driving.[244] Fuel is saved, and emissions reduced, by driving close to the optimum speed of 55-65 mph when allowable (keep an eye on your car's dashboard display if it can show the current mpg). Slow down - driving at 70 mph uses up to 15 per cent more fuel than at 50 mph. Accelerate and brake gently, keeping an eye on the road ahead so that you react in good time. Change up a gear at 2,500 rpm for petrol cars and 2,000 rpm for diesel cars. Don't let the engine idle - switch off the engine when stopped for more than ten seconds; many modern cars do this automatically. In addition to saving emissions and money, you are also being more considerate to people around you who are forced to breath in the emissions and listen to the noise of your engine for no good reason. Under-inflated tyres can increase fuel consumption by up to three per cent, so check their pressure regularly, particularly when the outside temperature changes (tyre pressure drops as air temperature falls and *vice versa*). Remove unnecessary loads, and take off the roof rack or roof box when not required, to minimise drag. Car heaters use excess heat from the engine and so don't consume extra fuel but air-conditioning increases fuel use at all speeds.

Step 3. Generating energy for low-carbon transport

Unlike electricity and heat, it is not immediately obvious how one can generate one's own 'renewable' energy for transport although walking and cycling can be presented as one form of self-generated low-carbon energy for transport over short distances.

How are you doing with your car mileage?

In 2014 the annual distance travelled by privately owned and company owned cars in England, for business, commuting and other private use, was 7,900 miles. On average petrol cars were driven 6,700 miles whereas diesel cars were driven 10,700 miles. (Data from Tables NTS0901 and NTS0903 at www.gov.uk/government/statistical-data-sets/tsgb09-vehicles).

The above figures are averages for England but give you some idea of the typical annual mileages of petrol and diesel cars. Perhaps they will encourage you to reduce the miles driven in your car(s).

A more realistic approach is the use of liquid biofuels which can take the place of fossil fuel petrol and diesel which individuals can chose to purchase if they are suitable for their vehicle and available. I mention biofuels here because, even though they cannot be grown by most drivers, they are a form of renewable energy. Biofuels are made from naturally grown materials after some chemical process that converts the raw material into a suitable fuel. Early examples were the conversion of rapeseed and palm oil to bio-diesel and the fermentation of sugars from maize (corn) to produce ethanol. But the lifecycle of such fuels depends on the growth rate of the feedstock and the amount of energy, land and water required to produce the fuel. These first generation biofuels were soon shown to be unsustainable because they require too much land and water and have a low energy return on energy invested (EROI; see Chapter 2 for a discussion of EROI). Research is going on to produce suitable transport fuels from grasses, woody crops, agricultural waste, and inedible oils and even from algae and synthetic biology techniques, because their EROI and demands for land and water appear to be more manageable.[245] It is likely that biofuels are a fuel of the future and, until they become commercially available and widespread, are likely to be overshadowed by hybrid vehicles, partly running on fossil fuels, and all-electric vehicles.[246]

Non-business travel and holidays abroad

This section is principally concerned with trips abroad, either for visiting friends or family or taking holidays. The carbon footprint of such trips is highly dependent on the distance and mode of transport. The emissions from just one return long-haul flight from London to Sydney, Australia, for example, is equivalent to about two fifths of the average UK citizen's carbon footprint in a year.

Jet aircraft burn a special type of fuel, usually a derivative of oil, which is rich in hydrocarbons. When jet fuel is burnt it emits not only water vapour and carbon dioxide but also other greenhouse gases, nitric oxide and nitrogen dioxide (usually described together as NOx), water vapour, particulates (soot and sulphate particles), sulphurous oxides, incompletely burned hydrocarbons and chemically active, so-called free radicals.[247] Since aircraft flying further than 400 kilometres cruise at over 9,000 metres altitude the exhaust emissions from their jet engines at that height have an impact on global warming which is greater than that of the emitted carbon dioxide alone.[248] This is true of all flights described as short-haul and long-haul.[249]

The water vapour, as a greenhouse gas, causes warming. Nitrogen oxides contribute to the formation of ozone, which leads to warming, but they also lead to a depletion of methane, another greenhouse gas, which thereby has a cooling impact. However, the net effect of NOx gases is one of warming. Water vapour and

141

soot can lead to the formation of cloud-like linear condensation trails (contrails), while sulphurous oxides, sulphuric acid and soot lead to an increase in the cirrus cloud cover. All these warming effects are real yet it is difficult to estimate the precise extra warming, and over what period it has an impact, in addition to that caused by carbon dioxide alone.[250] For that reason when estimating the climate impact of a jet aircraft some multiple of the CO_2 emissions is used. As noted in Chapter 4, different multiples have been proposed which are usually in the range of around two to four. The UK government's Department of Environment, Food and Rural Affairs (Defra) recommends that a factor of 1.9 times the CO_2 emissions is used but this may be conservative as higher factors are used by others.[249]

To come down to Earth so to speak, and to provide some benchmark figures, here are some examples of emissions from various return economy class flights from Heathrow Airport in London, calculated with the atmosfair calculator[251] and multiplied by 0.63 to allow for the difference between the multiplier of three used by atmosfair and Defra's recommended value of 1.9 (see table). Recall that the average carbon footprint from all sources of a UK citizen in 2013 was about 16.4 tonnes CO_2e.

Carbon footprints of some representative return, economy class, long-haul flights from Heathrow airport in London

Destination airport	Emissions per pass. (tonnes CO_2e)	Distance (km)	Emissions per pass.km (gCO_2e/km)
Dubai, UAE	1.7	11,086	246
New York, USA	1.8	11,172	256
Rio de Janeiro, Brazil	3.0	18,592	259

Los Angeles, USA	3.1	17,612	275
J'burg, S. Africa	3.5	18,238	303
Singapore	4.3	21,852	310
Sydney, Australia	6.5	34,530	317

From the table we can see that the effective emissions per passenger.kilometre range between 246 and 317 grams of CO_2e and increase with the length of the flight. Emissions increase with distance because the plane has to use more energy to carry the extra fuel required to fly further.

People's attitudes to flying and climate change are revealing. As an editorial in the scientific journal Nature said recently *"Aviation has become a symbol of the world's reluctance to make serious efforts to tackle climate change — perhaps unfairly, given its relatively slight (although growing) contribution to the global-warming problem. On an individual level, those who travel by air leave gigantic carbon footprints, governments continue to invest in runways and airports, and the industry remains focused on growth."* Some people, encouraged by airline advertising, look upon flying as a sign of status and their success in life. Others just seem unwilling to acknowledge the connection between their flights and climate change. A good friend, who is a scientist with an international reputation and who understands climate change, recently told me he was flying on a long weekend from the UK to continental Europe to visit family and then in the next breath he remarked on how the US National Aeronautics and Space Administration (NASA) had just announced that February 2016 had been the most abnormally hot month ever recorded and stated jocularly *"We are doomed"*. There is no doubt that the emissions from individuals' 'frequent flying', another form of status encouraged by airlines, can easily become the largest part of an individual's carbon footprint (see Chapter 3).

In 2014 the Department for Transport (DfT) conducted a survey of the UK public's experiences and views of flying.[252] Almost half of the people surveyed had flown in the last 12 months and a tenth had made four or more flights in that period. 37% of flights were short-haul and 18% were long-haul. People living in London and the South East were more than twice as likely to have taken a long-haul flight. The situation has been expressed in another way by Airport Watch, which describes itself as "*an umbrella movement uniting the national environmental organisations, airport community groups, and individuals opposed to unsustainable aviation expansion*", as "*15% of the UK population take 70% of all the flights*".[253]

A surprisingly large proportion of flights are for non-business purposes. In 2010 the percentage of passengers flying for leisure or, in roughly equal measure, to visit friends and family was 70.1% at Heathrow, 79.6% at Gatwick, 70.5% at Manchester, 80.4% at Luton and 82.3% at Stansted.[254] In other words, less than 30% of flights made from these airports were for business. The DfT survey also found that frequency of flying increases with income and socioeconomic group. Therefore it seems fair to conclude that better-off people are making a major contribution to emissions from flying from their propensity to fly more often for leisure and to visit friends and family.

So how do the flight emissions compare with other forms of transport that we might take to go on holiday? It should be obvious to any knowledgeable car owner that on a long-haul flight passenger aircraft emit far more per passenger than what their car might emit. In 2014 the average car in the UK was estimated, on the basis of manufacturers' figures, to emit 157 grams CO_2e per kilometre (say 180 grams per kilometre after a conservative 15 per cent uplift for real world driving as noted by the UK's Committee on Climate Change[255]) and the average new car emitted 125 grams CO_2e (144 grams after uplift).[256] Further, when there are two or three passengers in a car, although the extra load including luggage will increase its emissions slightly, this will not double or triple the emissions. Carrying passengers means the emissions per car occupant (or passenger.kilometre) will actually decrease proportionally.

No normal holiday maker is going to drive to Dubai let alone any of the other destinations in the table! So let's compare the emissions from travelling 1000 km by plane and car which should be a plausible, if very long, day's driving for most holiday makers. The RAC estimates that it takes about ten and a half hours of non-stop driving to travel the 1005 kilometres from London to Zurich.[257] On the basis of 180 grams CO_2e per kilometre a car with a driver and passenger (or co-driver) will emit a total of 181 kg CO_2e whereas two economy passengers in a plane will emit a total of 218 kg CO_2e (both one-way). Obviously four people flying will more than double the emissions compared to all four going by car (436 kg as against 181 kg – or a little more - of CO_2e).

That leaves going by train. Here I must admit some bias because, since the Eurostar service started under the English Channel in 1994, I have travelled all over Europe from London by high-speed train visiting places as far apart as Stockholm, Budapest, Bologna and Madrid and many other cities in between and found it to be an enjoyable, relaxing and reliable experience. In Europe high-speed trains travel at up to 360 km per hour (225 mph) and offer smooth, comfortable, city-centre to city-centre journeys.[258,259] One avoids the hassle of the airport check-in queue. There is space to move around the train at will without the constraints of seat belts. Train emissions can be significantly less than those of cars, let alone planes. Eurostar itself, the high-speed service from London St. Pancras International to the centres of Paris and Brussels, has low emissions partly because it uses low-carbon nuclear electricity on the sections within France. I can do no better than quote Mark Smith, the originator of the renowned Seat61 web site for worldwide train travel information, who says *"Taking the train to Paris instead of flying cuts CO_2 emissions per passenger not just by a measly 10% or 20% or even 50%, but by a staggering 90%..."* and that's without applying any correction for the effect of the plane's non-CO_2 emissions on global warming.[260] He quotes some savings relative to flying on other routes to the continent and none is less than 80 per cent.

An alternative, but possibly not widely accepted, view of the environmental impact of high-speed train versus aviation was presented by the European Regions Airline Association in a report published around 2012.[261] It is also worth recalling a warning made as long ago as 2004 that, apparently because of aerodynamic drag, a train's energy consumption per seat will increase threefold as its speed increases from 200 to 350 km per hour.[262] So, from the emissions point of view, high-speed trains also have their limitations although few of them today travel for most of their journey at anywhere near 350 km per hour (220 mph).

If you want to use a ready reckoner that compares the emissions of flights, trains and cars for journeys to, and within, the continent of Europe try the web site at www.uic.org/EcoPassenger-and-Ecotransit and click on the link for EcoPassenger.[263] The site calculates the carbon dioxide emissions per person (including optionally the non-CO_2 contribution to global warming by aircraft flying more than 500 km) and also the emissions of particulate matter, nitrogen oxides and non-methane hydrocarbons. Rather impractically the site always assumes that the car carries 1.5 'passengers', meaning occupants in this case, but this can easily be changed to a whole number! Not surprisingly the end result, as regards emissions, is always that the 'normally crowded' train is better than the car, even with four occupants, which is better than the plane.

Taking a holiday on a cruise ship, especially if it does not involve any flights, may seem like an environmentally friendly act. Today the largest cruise ships displace around 225,000 tonnes, not much less than the largest oil tankers, are 360 metre long and carry over 5,000 passengers.[264] They are like small floating cities. Cruise ships burn bunker oil, which has high sulphur content, and because the exhaust is so polluting there are restrictions in some Emission Control Areas, notably around North America, on what cruise ships can emit. Cruise ships may incinerate some of their solid waste, and discharge some of the remaining waste, and grey and sewage water, into the sea.[265]

Carnival is one of the world's largest cruise ship operators. In 2013 they carried 10.1 million passengers and their ships emitted around 10.6 million tonnes CO_2e implying an average footprint of 1 tonne CO_2e per passenger.[266] Given the lack of information available in the public domain it does not seem to be possible to arrive at a more accurate figure for Carnival's ships.

However, a detailed study of the CO_2 emitted by cruise ships visiting the Antarctic from South American ports obtained a median (approximate average) emissions figure of 0.25 tonnes CO_2 per passenger per day on trips lasting 16 to 20 days on cruise ships with a gross tonnage of 29,000 to 109,000 tonnes. This figure implies that emissions per passenger on such trips could be up to five times greater than those inferred from the average Carnival cruise. The figure also omits the extra emissions from the return flights to South America to join the cruise ship.[267] It appears that a holiday on a cruise ship may not be as low-carbon as one might hope.

Step 1. Suggestions for reducing the emissions involved in non-business travel and holidays abroad

The simplest suggestion is to **avoid flying** as much as you can, or even altogether. Mostly this may mean taking holidays closer to home although they can still be abroad. It can be argued that the countries that offer beaches, warm seas and sunshine, often the main attraction of flying to far-away places, need tourism to sustain their economies. This may be true if the infrastructure used by the tourists is owned by indigenous companies and not by some multinational hotel chain or other company based in another country, but it ignores the contribution of the tourists' flights to causing climate change. The countries that have the most overall vulnerability to climate change are in the tropics, mainly in Central America, Africa, the Middle East and Southeast Asia.[268] The countries that contribute least to greenhouse gas emissions today, yet are the most vulnerable to the negative effects of climate change, excepting the Middle East, are similarly located.[269] These countries are often attractive to the more affluent holidaymakers who are the target of this book. Flying to the Maldives or some idyllic Pacific atoll, or even to some Caribbean islands, will only help to seal the fate of its inhabitants some of whose homes will eventually be drowned beneath rising seas or be flattened in the next extreme tropical storm. Even countries outside the tropics, such as the UK, are not immune to the damaging effects of climate change, such as extreme weather events and rising sea level, as mentioned in Chapter 1.

Visiting family abroad is a rather special case sometimes described as generating 'love miles'. It is easy to understand the emotional pull of wanting to meet up with close family members instead of making do with Skype or similar video-conferencing arrangements. The only practical suggestion I can make is for the less numerous party to make the trip, so as to cut down on passenger.miles, to fly direct without stopovers (to avoid the emissions from extra landings and take-offs) and to make fewer but longer visits. If your destination is in North America or Australia consider flying to the airport closest to your departure country, such as New York in the USA or Perth in Western Australia if starting in the UK, and then travelling on by rail or coach from there.

Whether to travel on **holiday by high-speed train or car** is a personal decision that will depend on the country or countries being visited and other circumstances. Either mode of travel is an excellent way to see a country (and the countries *en route*) and can be a rewarding and fun part of the holiday experience. For minimum hassle you could choose the high-speed train and arrange to pick up a hire car on arrival at your destination to provide maximum flexibility for getting around. If your train journey is spread over two days and one night, in 36 hours from London you can be as far away as Budapest, Belgrade, Naples or Seville. You have the choice of either taking a sleeper compartment or couchette on the train or stopping over in a hotel on the way.

Taking a car ferry. If you choose to go to the continent by car your trip is likely to involve using either Eurotunnel's Le Shuttle under the Channel or a cross-Channel ferry. Eurotunnel claims that "*The Fixed Link is the most environmentally-friendly way of crossing the Channel*"; by 2010 they say they had reduced their emissions by over 55 per cent since starting operations. According to a study of Eurotunnel conducted in 2010 by logistics specialists JMJ Conseil, "*a truck that crosses the Strait of Dover through the Channel Tunnel generates on average 20 times less greenhouse gas than crossing by ferry.*"[270] Regular car ferries across the Channel are similarly reluctant to disclose the precise footprint of taking a car on board. One article in the Guardian newspaper in

149

2007 stated "*A standard car ferry emits just 10kg of CO_2 per foot passenger for a return trip Dover-Calais*". Another source quotes an anonymous independent study of ferry operators in Europe as finding that an average ferry causes the "*emission of 0.12kg CO_2 per passenger kilometre*" which is a good deal less than the average UK car.[271] For the shortest, 42-kilometre crossing from Dover to Calais this implies emissions of five kg CO_2e one-way, as also implied by the Guardian article, but the emissions will be strongly dependent on the speed of the ferry. If you take one of the ferries from UK to northern Spain a one-way trip in a medium sized car with two passengers and luggage will cause emissions of around 125 kg CO_2e.[272] If you drive overland the car emissions will be about 120 kg CO_2, depending on the size of the car, but this figure neglects emissions from any overnight stay in a hotel or B&B.

Step 2. Using energy more efficiently when on non-business travel and holidays abroad

This topic was dealt with above when discussing which modes of transport create the least emissions.

Step 3. Generating low-carbon fuel for aviation

Biofuels have been considered for use in aircraft and have been proposed by some as the primary means by which the aviation industry could reduce its carbon footprint. After a multi-year technical review by aircraft makers, engine manufacturers and oil companies, biofuels were approved for commercial use in aircraft in July 2011. Since then, some airlines have experimented with using biofuels on commercial flights. The focus of the industry has now turned to second generation sustainable biofuels (called sustainable aviation fuels or SAF) that will neither compete with food supplies nor will be major consumers of prime agricultural land or fresh water.[273] So far most biofuel-powered demonstration flights have used a blend of regular kerosene and biofuel. The sources of the biofuels included algae, used cooking oil and Jatropha, a flowering plant.[274] To be accepted, a SAF has to overcome various environmental and regulatory obstacles in order to achieve certification. In reality the use of biofuels to power commercial aircraft remains an interesting and expensive oddity that shows no sign at present of being taken up on a large scale.

Similarly, while research into solar, electric and hydrogen propelled aircraft is ongoing, it is not expected that any of these technologies will be feasible in the near or medium term due to aviation's need for high power-to-weight ratios and globally compatible infrastructure. The need for high power-to-weight ratios is determined by the physics of flight. Huge investment has been made in current airport infrastructure that supports the safe, efficient and prompt re-fuelling of aircraft, for example, as well as the delivery of fuel from oil refineries, and it would be very expensive to have to replace this with the infrastructure for a radically different fuel.

Summary

Frequent trips

- *Frequent, or even daily, trips include commuting to work, going to school and buying food.*
- *Step 1*
  - *In general, for shorter journeys, it is better to reduce emissions by walking, cycling or using public transport such as a bus. Using a car is the worst choice. For longer journeys, in order of increasing emissions, it is better to use a coach, train or a car with at least one passenger.*
  - *There is huge scope for reducing the number of trips by car and the distances travelled. These include more walking and cycling, homeworking and car sharing.*
- *Step 2*
  - *To reduce your personal emissions either get rid of your car altogether or change to a less carbon emitting, but possibly second-hand, car. If possible sell on the car you are replacing.*
  - *Buy and use a bicycle*
  - *Practise eco-driving*

Non-business travel and holidays abroad

- *Steps 1 and 2*
  - *The biggest source of emissions from non-business travel and holidays abroad is long-haul flying.*

Summary (continued)

- o *On holiday, avoid flying as much as you can. Where practical, driving, especially with one or more passengers, creates less emissions per head than flying. High-speed trains within Europe are even better. Ferries generally have low emissions but cruise ship holidays can increase your footprint substantially.*
- *Step 3*
  - o *Commercial aircraft will not fly regularly on low-carbon, renewable fuels for the foreseeable future.*

CHAPTER 9: EXAMPLES OF RETROFITTED AND NEW BUILD HOMES

In this chapter I am going to give a few examples of the low emissions that are achievable from retrofitting an existing home or from building a new home with a very high standard of insulation. But first I need to briefly review the legal, regulatory and planning implications of making changes to a home.

The legal situation, building regulations and local planning regulations

There are two issues to consider. The first is ownership of the home (whether it is freehold, leasehold or a short-term rental lease) and the second is building and planning regulations.

Clearly if you have freehold ownership of your home then you can decide what is done to it (subject to building and planning regulations and to your mortgage lender if you have one). But if you lease your home then you will need to communicate with your landlord. From April 2016, under the Energy Efficiency (Private Rented Property) (England and Wales) Regulations 2015 No. 962, landlords will not be able to refuse any reasonable requests from existing tenants to improve their property's energy performance. The regulations also prescribe a minimum level of energy efficiency and a landlord may not grant a new tenancy, or renew an existing tenancy, of a private rented property after 1st April 2018, or continue to let a domestic private rented property after 1st April 2020, where its energy performance falls below an Energy Performance Certificate level of E.[275] However homes in multiple occupancy appear to be excluded from these regulations. In addition there may be a let out for landlords, unless the whole cost of the improvement can be financed at no cost to the landlord, which seems to make a mockery of the whole objective of the regulations.[276]

Changes to a property obviously have to comply with the building regulations.[277] Planning regulations tend to vary from one local authority to another but planning permission is not normally required, for example, for fitting insulation or replacing doors or windows if no change in external appearance is involved.[278] The Planning Portal at www.planningportal.gov.uk/permission/ provides very helpful advice. If your home is listed or is in a conservation area you should consult your local planning authority.

Heat loss from homes

Most of the changes that save on emissions are to do with saving on heat losses in colder weather. The Royal Institute of British Architects (RIBA), in their Climate Change Tools package of guidance documents, points out that a home can gain and lose heat in several ways. Obviously heat is gained through the heating system but other contributions come from passive solar gain, cooking, lights and appliances, the occupants and the use of hot water. About half the heat is lost through the fabric of the home (roof, walls, floors and openings) but heat is also lost through ventilation and air leakage (about one third) and what are described as thermal bridges (about one fifth) which are points of low thermal resistance in the structure around junctions (such as gaps in the insulation) and openings.[279]

In my own case the retrofitting of our house was done on a gradual, *ad hoc* basis over several years, as mentioned in the Preface, and I shall start with that.

Our household

My wife and I moved into our detached house, which was built in the late 1980s, in December 1995. It had limited loft insulation, an unfilled cavity wall, a gas central-heating system with thermostatic radiator valves on the radiators and double glazing throughout which had only a five millimetre gap between the panes. In the first complete calendar year (1996) that we lived in the house we appear, on the basis of estimated meter readings, to have consumed around 3,200 kWh of electricity and 24,000 kWh of gas. We then started to carry out the Step 1 activities listed in earlier chapters to save energy but the greater savings came when we started a series of Step 2 and Step 3 changes spread out over the following years (for an explanation of these Steps see Chapter 5).

Following the installation of around 250 mm of loft insulation our electricity and gas consumption fell to around 2,450 and 18,000 kWh respectively the following year. In 2002 the cavity wall was filled with mineral wool insulation and gas consumption that year dropped to 16,000 kWh. In 2006 we fitted a hot-water solar panel but without any immediate substantial decrease in gas consumption although in subsequent years it was lower (there were teething problems in the first year). Incidentally we did not consider fitting photovoltaic panels because of a lack of suitable space with the right orientation and because of shading by trees.

From 2007, when we consumed 1,639 kWh of electricity and 14,225 kWh of gas, I kept detailed records of our gas and electricity consumption as well as our car mileage. Since 2007 it has proved impossible to cut our annual electricity consumption to much below 1,600 kWh (see first figure) even after changing over entirely to compact fluorescent lamps (CFLs) or LED light bulbs and low-energy screens on our two desk-top computers and our TV. Our current electricity consumption is also down to having a rather old (late 1980s), and poorly insulated, electric oven, a fridge/freezer (bought new in 2002) and a modern A+++ washing machine (we don't have a dishwasher). It corresponds overall to 9.3 kWh per square metre of floor space per year.

We've had more success with reducing our gas consumption (see first figure) following various improvements to the thermal insulation of the house. Gas consumption fluctuates with the local weather.[280] Calendar year 2010 was particularly cold in both winters, whereas 2011 was unusually warm as was December 2015. In early 2009 we replaced all the first floor windows with A-rated double glazing, which has a 22 mm gap between the panes, and this was repeated on the ground floor windows in summer 2012. In August 2011 we replaced our over 20-year old gas boiler with a condensing boiler which, together with the effect of the 2012 double glazing, led to a 30 per cent reduction in gas used between calendar years 2010 and 2013. Also in 2011 we replaced the front door, which had single-glazed panels and a draughty letter slot, with a composite door[281] with double glazed panels and no letter slot. Finally in 2015 we dry-lined (insulated) a wall, which had been built when we extended a room into a former garage space, and this greatly improved the temperature in the room. By 2015 our annual gas consumption was 40 per cent down on what it had been in 2007 and was equivalent to around 49 kWh per square metre of floor space.

Relative reductions in consumption of electricity and gas and car miles driven in our household (2007-2015)

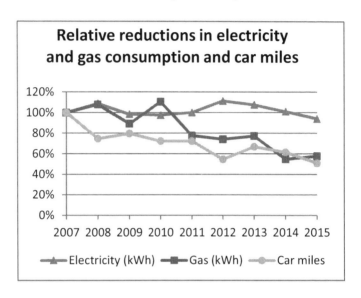

Relative reductions of emissions in our household (2007-2015)

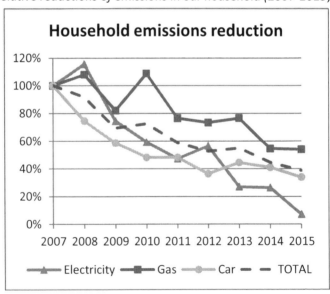

In 2007 the annual mileage of our only car, a 1400 cc petrol-engine model, was just under 12,000 miles. By dint of walking, cycling or using buses for almost all journeys in the town where we live and by being more economical with longer journeys, we have managed to reduce our annual mileage to between 6,000 and 7,000 miles which represents a reduction of 40-50 per cent compared to 2007.

But the real payback has been in reducing our carbon emissions. In the second figure I have used the electricity conversion factors which were provided by the company which now supplies us with electricity from 100 per cent renewable energy. So from 2015 the only CO_2 emissions are those associated with the transmission and distribution of electricity over the national grid giving a reduction of 93 per cent since 2007. For gas I used the DECC recommended conversion factors and this gives a saving in emissions of 46 per cent relative to 2007. Lastly in 2009 we changed our car from a 1400 cc petrol-engine car to a 1400 cc diesel-engine car with vastly reduced CO_2 emissions; the diesel car regularly achieves over 60 mpg on extra-urban journeys. Combined with the reduction in annual mileage this gave us a saving in the car's CO_2 emissions of 66 per cent. Thus overall our total annual household footprint from electricity, gas, car and public transport, including some holidays using high-speed trains on the continent, has been cut by 61 per cent since 2007 (see second figure) to around three tonnes of CO_2.

A major retrofit

My acquaintance Peter retrofitted the whole of his four-bedroom detached house, built in 1979, with the aim of saving at least 80 per cent of the consumed energy. When Peter started the retrofit in 2009 the house already had a standard insulated cavity wall, a condensing boiler and thermostatic radiator valves on all radiators. So he started at what was already quite a high standard

159

of energy efficiency and this was an ambitious target. He did not use an architect because no major structural changes were involved, but he had the help and on-call advice of a very experienced building supervisor, who assisted with producing drawings of the project. A builder provided bricklaying skills but Peter shared other tasks with him. Planning permission was required but the local planners raised no significant objections. Peter told me that it was also essential to have the support of the other house occupants because of the degree of disruption that such a major retrofit involves!

The first task was to carry out thorough research and draw up a very detailed plan (it must have helped Peter a good deal that he had been a professional project manager). For example, he had to plan to introduce underfloor pipework for rainwater harvesting which wasn't actually going to be connected up until a much later stage. Peter used the two-volume *Green Building Bible*[282] to guide him and to decide on the insulation and other specifications for the modified house.

This is not the place to give a blow by blow account of the different phases of the retrofit although I found it fascinating to spend time with Peter to learn about his project. What follows is a summary. He began by adding a ground floor extension, built to the desired high-specification, as a test of the retrofitting he was going to carry out elsewhere. This involved an extraordinarily well insulated floor with underfloor heating pipes and external walls with 200 mm of rigid foam insulation and 300 mm in the roof. The other external walls of the house have 110 mm of insulation and are rendered on the ground floor and tile hung above. The original suspended joist floor on the ground floor had to be re-laid with generous insulation. All living room radiators were removed. The original roof was insulated with 300 mm of rigid foam insulation under the rafters of the pitched roof. Photovoltaic and solar thermal panels were added to the roof. All windows were replaced with triple or double glazing and existing external doors were replaced by highly insulated doors. A wood-burning stove was fitted in the living area with dense concrete blocks at the sides and back to provide a large thermal mass, essentially to continue to provide heat after the stove had been extinguished. Warm air can also be piped upstairs when the living area gets too warm. The stove was designed to draw in external air directly from the outside without causing any indoor draughts. In any well insulated house it is essential to introduce fresh air to replace humid and oxygen-poor, but carbon dioxide-rich, air. This is done by having a constantly running 30W fan which sucks air out of the house through a heat exchanger (mechanical ventilation heat recovery or MVHR system) and draws in air, often naturally pre-warmed, from under the roof tiles.

The outcome of all this work, spread over seven years, was quite amazing. Peter managed to reduce his carbon emissions by 86 per cent, in other words his home now causes the emissions of less than one seventh of what it emitted at the outset. In 2014 gas consumption had been cut by 84 per cent to 2770 kWh. In 2014 electricity consumption had been cut by 41 per cent to 2500 kWh but, after allowing for zero-carbon electricity exported to the grid from the PV panels, the net consumption was as little as 300 kWh. Although heating demand is now minimal, and largely met by the wood-burning stove, electricity is still required for appliances, lighting, cooking and the air circulation fan, especially outside daylight hours when the PV panels cannot provide electricity. Rainwater harvesting, which is used for flushing toilets, washing clothes and outdoor activities, has meant that water consumption has been halved to 700-1000 litres per week which is a third to a half of the national average.

It should be no surprise that Peter's house is one of 200 SuperHomes in the UK chosen to demonstrate very low emissions living. If you are tempted to create a SuperHome too more information and advice can be found at www.superhomes.org.uk/.

Building a new home

Given the considerable savings that can be made from a concerted effort to save energy by retrofitting, even lower emissions should be achievable from building a new home from scratch. It has always amazed me that in the late 20th century houses were still being built by laying one 8¼ inch by 2½ inch brick on top of another. This is a technology not much different from the sun-dried bricks that were used in the Middle East almost 10,000 years ago and the bricks from mobile kilns supposedly used by the Roman legions about 2000 years ago![283] Since about the year 2000 more homes have been built using the method of off-site construction or prefabrication in which large wall panels and other structural elements are made under cover in modern and highly automated factories. This means that the finished products can be made to a consistent standard with less waste and disruption, fewer defects and accidents and that construction on site can proceed much more quickly, even within days.[284] Some homes built in this way have timber frames which, from the environmental point of view, are to be encouraged since the design locks up carbon in the timber for the lifetime of the building.

Standards are very important too to ensure that new homes are as energy efficient as possible. There are cost implications here as well of course. Developers like to maximise their profit, sometimes with little regard for the eventual energy demand of the occupied home. This happens even though in the long run it will be environmentally better to make the home marginally more expensive to buy by applying higher standards and/or including extra features. And finally, as we saw in Chapters 6 and 7, energy demand is to some extent determined by the occupants and their understanding of the heating system they can control and the way they use electrical appliances.

Unfortunately, the history of building standards in UK homes in recent years reflects no credit on government. Besides the Building Regulations, which set a minimum standard for all new homes, a Code for Sustainable Homes (CSH) was set up in 2007 as a voluntary standard for England, Wales and Northern Ireland. The Building Research Establishment (BRE) describes the Code as an environmental assessment method for rating and certifying the performance of new homes (although at least one example exists of Code Level 6 being applied to a retrofitted home).[285] The Code was developed by BRE Global, a subsidiary of BRE, but it was a UK Government owned standard. The Code has various levels from Level 1 up to Level 6 (the highest standard) which specify the allowable emissions against nine criteria. The objective was to construct buildings at Level 6 with net zero carbon dioxide emissions by 2016. However, the government started to dismantle the CSH in March 2015 and it has now been replaced by BRE's Home Quality Mark (HQM) which can be applied to all new homes built in the UK. Under this scheme independent, fully trained, licensed professionals will assess and score a new home on a wide range of criteria that fall under the three headings of running cost, wellbeing of the occupants and the embodied and operational carbon footprint of the home. An important aspect of the HQM appears to be that the scoring is done after the building has been completed and not from the plans or from estimates.

Unfortunately, the HQM is a comparatively new standard and it is also voluntary and not backed up by any national legislation. Today the Building Regulations 2016 Part L1A *Conservation of fuel and power in new dwellings* are the principal statutory regulations that apply to all new homes with regard to their energy efficiency. Part L1B applies similarly to when changes are made to existing dwellings.[286]

163

A low-energy new build home

I now describe an example of a recently built home with low energy consumption. Jim and Angela and their two young children live in a detached house built in 2013 in a road with bungalows on one side and semi-detached houses on the other. I had observed the construction of their house several times in passing and was curious to know more and how happy they were with their new home. When I knocked on their door one sunny spring evening they were very welcoming and invited me in to talk about their home.

The bungalow which originally stood on the site was demolished. They engaged an architect who was given an outline specification to design a low-energy, air-tight house with four bedrooms and an open plan ground floor. Although originally they had considered aiming at a Code Level 4 standard this appeared to be too onerous because it included the disposal of rubble from the pre-existing bungalow and they focussed instead on the low energy consumption of the new house.

The architect decided to place the house to one side of the site with a north-south ridge at right-angles to the road. This effectively created a larger single area of garden than would have been the case if the building had been placed centrally. The foundations consist of 300 mm of rigid expanded polystyrene foam on which concrete was laid. This design limits heat loss by conduction from the building itself through its base into the ground. By thermally isolating the building's foundation from the ground I was told the energy performance of the building is improved as are the occupants' comfort levels and the management of moisture in the building.

A specialist builder constructed a timber-framed house which arrived as a kit of precisely manufactured and labelled components ready for assembly. The frame was clad externally in wooden sheet and an air-tightness test was conducted which revealed an excellent measurement of 1.2 $m^3/(h.m^2)$.[287] Batts of insulation were then installed internally between the vertical wall timbers and the roof joists and the walls were covered in plaster board.

The ground floor of the house is heated by a gas condensing boiler and underfloor pipes. There are no radiators on the first floor and just a heated towel rail in the bathroom. Because the thermal insulation is so effective Jim and Angela find their home is very comfortable with a low demand for heating. They consume about 3200 kWh of gas per year with the room thermostat set to a relatively high 21°C. The ground floor has large double-glazed windows on the west side which allow the underlying concrete base, acting as a thermal mass, to warm up in the afternoon and release heat in the evening. However passive solar gain is sometimes rather high in summer and so temporary external fabric blinds are used on some windows. A solar thermal panel provides about half the hot water needs of the family.

Because the building is so air tight mechanical ventilation heat recovery is used and this continuously changes the air every three hours while minimising the loss of heat. Jim told me that this keeps the air in the house fresh and means that clothes dry faster than they would otherwise.

Electricity is taken from the grid. There are no photovoltaic panels because the roof does not provide a southerly aspect. Annual electricity consumption for cooking, LED lighting, appliances and the ventilation system running 24 hours a day is around 2370 kWh.

A Passivhaus home

In recent years energy efficient homes have been constructed to other standards which were initially developed on the continent of Europe. Perhaps the most well known is the Passivhaus standard. It was developed in Germany in the early

1990s by Professors Bo Adamson of Sweden and Wolfgang Feist of Germany and the first dwellings to be completed to the Passivhaus standard were constructed in Darmstadt in Germany in 1991. The Passivhaus aim is to build a house that has an excellent thermal performance, and exceptional air-tightness with mechanical ventilation. Because of the high thermal insulation a traditional heating system is no longer considered essential. The annual heating demand of a Passivhaus building is less than 15 kWh per square metre of floor area meaning that annual fuel costs are reduced by a factor of at least five.[288] The Passivhaus Trust says *"Evidence and feedback to date shows that Passivhaus buildings are performing to standard, which is crucial, given that the discrepancy between design aspiration and as-built performance for many new buildings in the UK can be as much as 50-100%."* [289] The Trust estimates that globally 30,000 houses have been built to the standard.

In the UK over 250 Passivhaus buildings of all types had been completed and certified by the end of 2013. So it was with mounting excitement that I went to meet Ella in her home in a small village in the South Downs where she lives with her young family in one of the rare UK examples of a certified Passivhaus.

Ella and her husband have a background in town planning and so they began their project with the advantage of knowing how to approach and present their plans to local planners. They started from a hand-drawn scheme, designed to look like a barn conversion to blend in well with their rural surroundings. Following the granting of planning permission the hand-drawn design was then converted into formal plans by an architect. In turn the plans were checked for compliance with the Passivhaus standard by an energy specialist. Finally a third party checked the calculations to ensure, for example, that thermal bridging at key points, such as under the eaves and where the walls meet the foundations, and the triple glazing were likely to be up to the Passivhaus specification.

The next step in carrying out their new build was to find a builder who was comfortable with working to the strict Passivhaus standards. This was not easy because they found that many UK builders are conservative in their approach to, and lack knowledge of, non-traditional modes of construction. The breakthrough for Ella and her husband came when they attended the annual Ecobuild exhibition in London and found a specialist builder who was used to constructing bespoke homes. Even so, many components of the building had to be sourced from the continent. Although the engineered wooden frame of the building was of UK design it had to be cut under computer control in a factory in Germany and imported as a kit ready for assembly. This process minimises waste. The air handling unit is also German, the windows are Danish and the foundation system is a Swedish design installed by a Swede. But the wooden floors were parquet bought online on eBay and installed by an Englishman!

The house is built on a foundation composed of a layer of mixed clay, gravel, and sand (hoggin) which is somewhat permeable to water. 400 mm of reinforced polystyrene were laid on the hoggin with a concrete layer on top of that. The concrete is not designed to provide a thermal mass. The wooden pine frame is strengthened by spine beams made of glued laminated timber (glulam) and timber I-beams. The frame is covered on the outside by proprietary, tongue-and-grooved membrane sheets, for air tightness, and clad with oak planks above a low brick cladding. Finally a proprietary insulation, made from cellulose fibre from recycled newspaper, was blown into the 400 mm cavities between the studs in the frame. The roof is composed of clay tiles underlain by 400mm of the same insulation encased in the membrane sheet used elsewhere.

A Mechanical Ventilation and Heat Recovery (MVHR) system is an integral part of the house design. It removes stale warm air from the home and transfers heat from the warm outgoing air to the incoming cooler air. All the vents, one per room, and pipework required are out of sight within the fabric of the building. The MVHR system normally runs 24 hours a day and consumes around 40W.

Perhaps the most interesting part of my visit was to hear first-hand from Ella how one has to live in a Passivhaus home. She said that the house regulates its temperature with little input from the occupants. The indoor temperature is designed to be 21°C with a thermostat able to call for extra heat only if this temperature falls below 19°C, which it rarely does even with extreme night-time lows. On the rare occasions when a boost of heat is required this is provided by a small electrical heater in the MVHR system. During my visit on a sunny day many windows were slightly open to encourage a flow of cooler air through the house to prevent overheating.

Normally heat from the MVHR system and the occupants themselves, plus some contribution from cooking and various appliances, is enough to maintain the house at the required temperature. Although the house faces south passive solar gain is not excessive because of the triple glazing. Internal blinds were installed in a single, southwest facing bedroom. The home has a wood-burning stove. Living in the country makes it easy to find sources of logs, but there is a knack to getting the stove to draw properly when first lit because the MVHR system can suck smoke out of the stove!

I was told that there are very few disadvantages to living in a Passivhaus. The family found that the air could get rather dry (this was previously described as an advantage by Jim and Angela for drying washing in their home) but a more sophisticated and expensive MVHR system could have better controlled humidity.

On the rare occasions when there has been a power cut the occupants have become quite drowsy from the eventual build-up of carbon dioxide (because the house is so airtight and the MVHR system has shut off) but even if this happens during the night hours it is not seen to be a serious hazard to health. Apparently cut flowers and bananas also suffer from the lack of a diurnal temperature cycle because the house maintains itself at a constant temperature all day long!

I asked Ella why, recognising that only around 250 had been built so far, more homes were not being built to Passivhaus standard in the UK? Her opinion was that there was insufficient government pressure through regulations or other means and that many builders are resistant to such challenging designs. She quoted the examples of some parts of Austria and many towns and cities in Germany where all new and retrofitted public buildings have to be built to this standard. The Passivhaus standard is also mandatory in parts of Belgium, Ireland, Luxembourg, Norway and Spain.[290]

There may also be a misconception that building to the Passivhaus standard is more expensive than a traditional new-build but I was told that, provided the expert advisors were chosen carefully to have the right skills and the builder too was experienced, it should cost no more. Indeed, when the lack of capital outlay on radiators and a boiler and near-zero operating costs are factored in, it might even be cheaper. It was estimated that the 4-bedroom detached house I visited cost around £273,000 to construct and has an annual electricity demand, for the ventilation fan, of about 420 kWh per year. On the other hand an average UK home uses 4,170 kWh of electricity in a year, plus 14,829 kWh of gas![291]

Further information about Passivhaus homes can be found in the Passivhaus Handbook[292] and online at the Passivhaus Trust[293] and Green Building Store.[294]

Comparison of annual energy use in four different types of home

It is now useful to draw together some conclusions from the four examples of retrofitted or new-build homes described above. The table presents the main statistics for recent consumptions of gas and electricity of the four homes plus, for comparison, the average UK domestic consumption figures for 2013.[291]

The first thing to note is the very strong correlation between gas consumption, primarily for heating, and insulation. Not surprisingly the Passivhaus home, which has the highest insulation, uses no gas at all and the Average UK home uses the most, with the other homes consuming intermediate amounts according to their degree of insulation. It was estimated that in July 2013, of the approximately 25 million homes in the UK, about 68 per cent of homes with lofts had at least 125 mm of insulation, well below the recommended 270 mm of mineral wool, and 70 per cent of homes with cavity walls had cavity insulation.[295] Although there is a range of room thermostat temperature settings in the table the conclusion must be that thermal insulation, and that includes eliminating draughts, is the prime factor in determining the energy consumption and the carbon footprint of home heating.

A second conclusion is that electricity consumption is quite variable. For example, the electricity emissions from the 'SuperHome' and the 'Low-energy new build' are about 60 per cent of the 'Average UK home' whereas the emissions from the 'Retrofitted ad hoc' home are just 37 per cent of this figure. Although this is a tiny sample my hunch is that electricity use in a home is more a reflection of the lifestyle of the occupants, such as their use of a dishwasher, tumble drier, television or freezer, the number of appliances in the home and even of the self-discipline of the occupants depending on whether they regularly turn off the lights in unoccupied rooms or any appliances that are left on standby.

A DECC report in 2015 shows that electricity consumption for lighting and cooling has decreased since the early noughties and for cooking and home computing it has more or less plateaued. By 2013 there had been a steady increase for many years in the consumption by 'wet' appliances and consumer electronics, with the latter sector being at least 60 per cent higher than most of the others.[296] Although this report shows that the average domestic consumption of electricity has declined very slightly since 2008 in detail it suggests that we should reduce our use of dishwashers and even washing machines (the 'wet' appliances) and entertainment products and general gadgetry (the consumer electronics).

Comparisons of electricity and gas consumption and emissions in different homes

Home type	Gas (kWh)	Gas emissions (kg CO_2e) **	Electricity (kWh)	Electricity emissions (kg CO_2e) **	Energy by floor area+ (kWh/m^2)
1	14,829	2,735	4,170	2,085	Not known
2	8,220	1,516	1,540	771	59
3	*2,770	511	2,500	1,251	36
4	3,200	590	2,370	1,186	25
5	0	0	***420	***210	++ca. 14

Home types:
1. Average UK home[291], occupants unknown, room thermostat setting unknown
2. Retrofitted *ad hoc*, retired couple, room thermostat 17.5°C
3. SuperHome, retired couple, room thermostat 18°C

4. Low-energy new build, couple with 2 young children, room thermostat 21°C

5. Passivhaus, couple with 2 young children, room thermostat 21°C

Key to symbols in table:

* gas rarely used; main heating is by wood stove.

** calculated using DECC's conversion factors (all scopes) for 2015

*** for the MVHR alone. Consumption by appliances, lighting, cooking etc. is not available

\+ floor area estimated from planning applications if not otherwise available

\+\+ assuming 2,500 kWh for appliances

The results of a detailed survey of electrical appliances in homes in Leicester in 2009-2010 agree with the DECC report. The authors reported that previous research had already shown that the top quarter of homes, ranked by household income, consume almost half of the electricity in the whole domestic sector. The survey concluded that *"households which owned more than 30 appliances were significantly more likely to be high electricity consumers"*. Unsurprisingly the survey results also indicated that electricity consumption correlated with the number of occupants and the presence of children and teenagers.[297] Assuming that many electrical appliances are shared within a household (dishwasher, washing machine, lawn mower, oven, toaster etc.) and that the rest are often used by individuals, but mostly one appliance at a time, the fact that the number of appliances correlates with electricity consumption suggests that the problem is not the total number of appliances in use at all but the number of appliances that unnecessarily are left on or on stand-by.

The last column in the table presents an estimate of the annual electricity and gas consumed per unit of floor area. This is a useful metric for comparing energy consumption in homes of different sizes. It shows that in spite of my efforts to reduce energy consumption in my own home the overall results that I have achieved, although significant, fall far short of what can be achieved in a new build home (my home is about four times more energy intensive compared to a Passivhaus).

Summary

- *How alterations may be made to a home will depend on the ownership (freehold, leasehold or rental) and on having to comply with building and planning regulations.*

- *Landlords cannot now refuse any reasonable request from a tenant to improve their property's energy performance.*

- *Retrofitting a home can help to achieve significant savings in energy use and emissions particularly for heating. Some of it can be done by an experienced DIYer. It can be carried out in stages.*

- *A specially designed, new-build home can use even less energy than a retrofitted home and does not necessarily cost more but requires careful planning and execution.*

- *In the UK the Code for Sustainable Homes has been replaced by the voluntary Home Quality Mark.*

- *The highest standard today is that offered by Passivhaus whose accredited homes use almost no fuel for heating.*

- *Electricity consumption appears to depend on lifestyle and the occupants' behaviour as well as on the number of appliances in a household. It does not appear to relate to the degree of home insulation.*

CHAPTER 10: SOME HOME ECONOMICS

My arguments and discussion so far have been founded on the principle that reducing one's personal carbon footprint is more important than considering the actual cost of doing so. I have written about the various ways in which we can measure and reduce our carbon emissions with hardly any mention of cost. This was intentional. Underlying the text so far has been the assumption that those who are better off can afford, sooner rather than later, to spend on the actions required to significantly cut their emissions. My currency has been kilograms of emitted carbon dioxide and not pounds sterling. I am not an economist or an accountant but I can put off no longer some discussion of the financial implications of cutting carbon in the home and from our lifestyles. This explains my choice of title for this chapter.

Is a project worthwhile?

Let's suppose that we are considering spending money on a project such as the installation of solar PV panels on a roof. How should we decide whether this is going to be 'worthwhile'? Immediately we have a problem. Does 'worthwhile' involve only monetary considerations or should it include an environmental or even moral dimension such as a measure of the impact of our investment on climate change as a whole? And how should such aspects be quantified or even costed?

From a monetary viewpoint we can estimate whether, when and to what extent we shall make a profit or a loss from our investment. For example, how soon will the initial outlay on installing the PV panels be repaid by the savings made on the electricity not taken from the national grid? This estimate may also include some consideration of alternative ways in which the money might have been invested as well as the income from government feed-in tariffs.

However, this approach entirely avoids consideration of the environmental impact of our investment. We can, for example, calculate the likely reduction in greenhouse gas emissions from the electricity saved over the approximately 25-year lifetime of the PV panels. For completeness such a calculation should also include the emissions involved in the manufacture and installation of the panels. A proper, so-called life-cycle, assessment of the panels would therefore include the energy (and generated emissions) used to extract and refine the metals used in the panels and to grow the silicon crystals, which convert sunlight to electricity, plus the energy involved in creating the ancillary electrical wiring, inverters and other equipment and the transport of the raw materials and the finished product.

To complete the financial calculation we might also want to consider the importance of acting now to mitigate climate change, given that climate scientists insist that urgent action is required to keep global warming below at least 2°C, against putting off our investment into the future. This approach recognises that there is a cost involved in **not** tackling climate change today. In other words there is a cost associated with our continued use of electricity generated in a fossil-fuel burning power station because of the damage that is, and undoubtedly will be, caused by the associated emissions. Such a calculation is hard to do. As Lord Stern, the economist and principal author of the renowned 2006 report on *The Economics of Climate Change*, wrote recently *"The political will to make the necessary decisions depends partly on improving the analysis and estimates of the economics of climate change. Then the consequences of unmanaged global warming can be weighed much more transparently against the investments and innovations necessary to mitigate it."*[298] He goes on to describe how, in principle, models can estimate the incremental change in, or damage to, global economic output resulting from 1 tonne of man-made CO_2 or equivalent emissions and how such estimates can be used by policymakers in cost–benefit analyses of climate-change-mitigation policies. Such models can also be used to estimate the costs of climate change mitigation. Lord Stern ends by acknowledging that current models are insufficient to provide policy makers with the information they need.

In conclusion, it is evidently hard or impossible for the ordinary, better-off person to decide in an objective way whether their project is going to be 'worthwhile'. This is because how worthwhile an investment in emissions reduction will be can be presented in many different ways and the answer to the question can be chosen almost according to the desired outcome. This is not quite in the class of 'lies, damned lies and statistics' but one does wonder whether, for the better-off homeowner, it is simpler and just better to get on with an emissions reduction project and bathe afterwards in the warm glow of having done something right towards mitigating climate change and benefitting society in general. Just do it. If subsequently you can measure a reduction in your energy consumption, for example, then you can equate that quantitatively with a certain reduction in your emissions.

A financial incentive, such as a feed-in tariff, may well tip the balance for some people who are considering initiating a project. Nevertheless it is recognised by those who study human behaviour that it is easier to persuade someone to adopt 'helpful behaviour', in this case mitigating climate change or saving energy, who acts for reasons of bringing benefit to their family, friends or community than someone who acts to impress others or for personal financial gain. Almost everyone will hold values that fall in both camps but the key factor here is for the first (intrinsic) values to be seen to be more important that the second (extrinsic) values in the context of tackling climate change.[299]

Pitfalls to avoid when spending your savings

Let's now assume that by investing in a project in our home, such as improved insulation, or by changing our behaviour in some way, such as reducing our annual car mileage, that we have been able to cut our energy bills and therefore make a financial saving. Does it matter what we then do with our savings assuming that we spend them?

The emphatic answer is yes, absolutely. This is because, unless we save them for a rainy day, we should not aim to spend the savings in such a way that completely offsets the reduction in emissions that was achieved in the first place. For example, it would be pointless, from a climate change perspective, to spend the savings made over a year on flying to some attractive continental European city for the weekend. The emission from the flight could easily exceed the emissions saved. For example, a 3,000 kWh saving on your gas heating bill is equivalent to saving around 600 kg of CO_2 emissions. But a couple flying from London to Rome, Berlin or Prague and back would cause emissions of 777, 557 or 575 kg CO_2, respectively.[300]

The effect of spending on capital items is more difficult to judge because the carbon footprint of the item is not always published by the manufacturer (but you could ask them). A Dell Latitude E6400 laptop, for example, has a footprint of 320 kg CO_2e which is equivalent to 1600 kWh off your gas bill or 640 kWh off your electricity bill.[301] If you can't find the relevant figure for the item you want to buy you could refer to Michael Berners-Lee's book *How bad are bananas?* which was mentioned earlier.[302] Any item with a footprint of ten kg or less can count as low carbon but items with larger footprints include a pair of leather shoes, a night in a hotel, a leg of lamb and the annual use of a mobile phone. There are also arguments to be made for buying second-hand goods because no extra emissions are attributable to the new owner from the change of ownership. Buying second-hand avoids the embodied emissions attached to any brand new item.

A final example of how savings can be 'misspent' is when a homeowner changes to a cheaper energy supplier, something that we are constantly advised to do, yet ends up using more 'cheaper' energy, and therefore causing more emissions, than before. Someone who buys a more energy efficient car, that also emits less greenhouse gas per mile (CO_2 per kilometre), and consequently increases their annual mileage falls into the same category.

The above examples are all instances of what is known as the 'rebound effect'. This is a result that causes the net effect of emissions reduction actions to be less than expected or desired. These effects have been widely studied. The direct rebound effect occurs where increased efficiency and an associated cost reduction for a product or service results in its increased consumption because it is cheaper. The indirect rebound effect occurs where savings from efficiency and cost reductions enable more income to be spent on other products and services. One such study, which summarised earlier estimates of direct and indirect rebound effects in UK households, found that in some cases the rebound effects in areas such as food, heating, travel, transport, utilities and electricity could exceed 50 per cent[303] although smaller values, typically 27-37 per cent, for European households were presented in a report by the European Environment Agency.[304] A 50 per cent rebound effect means that the actual emissions savings were half of what they had been expected to be. If the rebound effect exceeds 100 per cent this is described rather dramatically as 'backfire' although the reality of the existence of backfire is said not to be supported by recent studies.[304]

Nevertheless, the authors of the study of UK households concluded that, when considering seven measures, *"Our main*

179

finding is that the rebound effects from these measures are in the range 5–15%, ... The primary source of these rebound effects is the re-spending of the cost savings on non-energy goods and services, and the primary reason the estimated effects are modest is that these goods and services are much less GHG [greenhouse gas] *intensive than energy consumption itself.*" They also state that studies of less greenhouse gas intensive areas of energy consumption, such as travel by road vehicle and food consumption, have typically found larger rebound effects.

So, as homeowners and individuals, we have to be aware of the rebound effect and how it may erode any savings in emissions that we are hoping to make. In the next section I shall explore how we can minimise or even largely avoid the rebound effect by spending on non-energy goods and services which are much less greenhouse gas intensive than energy consumption itself, as noted in the last paragraph.

Alternative ways to spend your savings

Goods and services that are relatively energy intensive are easier to identify and some have been mentioned above. They include taking flights, staying in upmarket hotels, buying goods that have been flown large distances or food that has a relatively large carbon footprint (such as red meat, including some beef and lamb,[305] and dairy products[306]). Goods that have been flown large distances may include consumer products (fashion goods, textiles, footwear and goods required to meet product deadlines such as publication of a Harry Potter book and the launch of Apple's iPhone 5) and perishable goods such as some flowers, vegetables, fish, meat and fruit. If you are unsure of the mode of transport used to import something you are about to buy why not ask in the shop? They should know or at least be able to find out from their supplier. Only about 1 per cent of internationally traded goods are transported by air but this small proportion accounts for about 40 per cent of their value.[307]

An alternative approach is to spend more money on goods or services that also help us to minimise our impact on the environment. For example, if you buy a brand-new item ensure that it is of the highest quality that you can afford so that it will last for many more years than an equivalent but cheaper item. For travel, an obvious example is the decision to take a high-speed train service within the UK, or from the UK to a destination elsewhere in Europe, instead of flying. In many instances, airlines do not pay fuel duties or ticket taxes on their international services[308] and therefore train fares tend to be relatively more expensive yet in emissions terms trains are the obvious choice as explained in Chapter 8.

Non-energy goods and services mean goods and services that do not obviously incur the expenditure of significant amounts of energy, or the creation of emissions, in their provision. There is in fact no end to the opportunities on offer to spend in this way.

Non-energy goods could include craft products (although pottery will normally have required the use of an electricity-hungry kiln relying on a fossil-fuel powered power station) such as drawings, paintings, hand-made fabrics, carvings and sculptures which are bought for their intrinsic beauty and the pleasure that they give the owner. Examples of non-energy services might include going to local concerts, plays or sports events, taking lessons in playing a musical instrument or sport, taking part in sports, joining an adult or higher education class or studying for an academic or vocational qualification. In all these cases we are paying for the time and skills of individuals who lead an activity in which we participate and not for energy itself.

Our use of time

The individual's use of time outside work, and the greenhouse gas emissions associated with different activities, have been studied too. This is an alternative approach to considering what goods and services to buy or what technology to use to reduce one's carbon footprint. Angela Druckman and others from the University of Surrey in UK found that leisure activities, both at home and outside the home, are generally associated with lower carbon emissions than non-leisure activities.[309] As these authors point out, we all have an allocation of 24 hours in every day and it is up to us to decide how we share the time between different activities. Besides sleep and rest, and ignoring commuting to work (discussed in Chapter 8), the other main categories were leisure and recreation, household maintenance (cleaning etc.) and food and drink. The latter two categories had considerably higher greenhouse gas intensities, defined in this case as the emissions per hour, than leisure and recreation. The activities with the highest greenhouse gas intensities are personal care, including clothes, clothes washing and health care, and eating and drinking, including eating out and alcohol. This conclusion appears to suggest that we should concentrate on less ironing, clothes washing and eating out and drink less alcohol. Leisure activities in and around the home have the lowest intensities beaten only by getting more sleep!

Investments

Another way to spend money which is directed to reducing emissions is to invest in renewable energy projects. It seems reasonable to assume that in the near future the generation and consumption of renewable energy will largely replace energy, and emissions, generated from fossil fuels. There are many examples in the UK, and elsewhere, of projects that seek funds from investors mainly for solar PV arrays (solar farms) and onshore wind turbines. Some of these are not-for-profit cooperative or community enterprises. One such organisation, Energy4All, states on its web site *"Energy4All was formed in 2002 to expand community ethical ownership of renewable energy. We now have 20 projects in the Energy4All family with 13,000 + members - £40m + raised through ethical investment enabling many more communities to benefit from renewable energy."* But they warn *"As unregulated share offers, investments do not receive the protection of the Government's Financial Services Compensation Scheme and investors do not have recourse to the Financial Ombudsman Service."* These are long-term investments either in the form of shares, which cannot be traded on the stock market, or bonds which provide a fixed interest income over a number of years. At the present time many such investments appear to give a better return than more conventional, but less risky, means.

Supporting a charity

Several international and national organisations have tackling climate change as a principal objective. The reason for listing several of these organisations here is that they all depend on funding support from their members and/or the general public. More details can be found on their web sites.

350.org, a non-profit organization in the USA, was founded by author Bill McKibben and others around 2008. It says it is building a global climate movement. Its online campaigns, grassroots organisation, and mass public actions are coordinated by a global network active in over 188 countries. It gets its name from the target of reducing global carbon dioxide levels in the atmosphere back to the 'safe' level of 350 ppm. Its most recent activity was a campaign in May 2016 to *Break Free from Fossil Fuels* by keeping coal, oil and gas in the ground.[310]

Avaaz (meaning 'voice' in several languages) says it is a global web-based movement with over 44 million members to bring people-powered politics to decision-making everywhere. It has been described, not surprisingly, as the globe's largest and most powerful online activist network. It campaigns through creating online petitions on numerous topics, which include climate change, but also funds media campaigns and direct actions, and emails, calls and lobbies governments, and organises 'offline' protests and events. In September 2014 it coordinated the 'biggest climate march in history'.[311]

In the UK, Friends of the Earth is a recognised charity and member of Friends of the Earth International which has groups in more than 75 countries. Climate change is among their campaigns. They are working on a strong global climate agreement, keeping fossil fuels in the ground, using energy efficiently and sparingly, creating a revolution in renewable energy and preparing for the unavoidable consequences of climate change.[312]

Also in the UK the 'Campaign against climate change' campaigns on topics related to climate change such as aviation, fracking and coal. It works with a wide range of local groups.[313]

Greenpeace is known for their members taking direct action around the world. They have a section in the UK. Their web site says *"Climate change isn't inevitable. We have the knowledge, skills and technologies to get ourselves out of this difficult situation. All over the world people have woken up to the threat, and are working to reduce the use of fossil fuels, stop rainforest destruction and get power from clean energy. Still much more needs to be done."*[314]

Lastly, I should mention the Centre for Alternative Technology (CAT) in Machynlleth, mid-Wales which recently celebrated its fortieth anniversary. CAT is a charity which offers visitors a marvellous array of display panels on energy saving and renewable energy and runs a graduate school offering a series of practical postgraduate courses at Masters degree level. One of its major projects is a series of reports on Zero Carbon Britain, mentioned in Chapter 2, which propose how Britain could become a zero carbon country.[315]

There are undoubtedly other organisations tackling climate change on a national or even an international scale but I have listed those most in the news.

Helping to slow population growth

Another aspect of humanity's greenhouse gas emissions and how they contribute to climate change, which so far I have not mentioned, is the impact of a growing global population. Clearly, in current circumstances, the more people that live on our planet the more energy they will use and the more emissions will be produced. In addition, as the global population grows, greater stress is put on natural systems globally and this might include the destruction of forests, which presently act as carbon sinks, to provide land on which to grow more food. There is no doubt that global population and greenhouse gas emissions have increased more or less in parallel in the 20th century. Population growth has been greatest in developing countries, yet the majority of emissions have come from the developed industrialised world. On the other hand, looking to the future, the growing population in the developing world will become the consumers of tomorrow as standards of living rise and they will contribute substantially to global greenhouse gas emissions if fossil fuels continue to provide the main sources of primary energy. Fortunately, there is evidence to suggest that birth rates decrease as higher standards of living are reached[316] but this will only work to reduce global emissions if at the same time the higher standard of living is achieved by a proportionately lower increase in emissions. In fact, in some developed countries there is concern that as birth rates fall there will be, or already are, socioeconomic problems related to support of the aged and the collection of taxes to cover the cost of providing pensions and other services.

185

For the above reasons the Population-Health-Environment Policy and Practice Group of USAID, the United States Agency for International Development, has stressed the importance of establishing population programmes - those that address unmet needs for reproductive health services around the world - which can slow the rate of population growth, and therefore be part of a long-term strategy to reduce global greenhouse gas emissions.[317] It is said that population programmes are easy to implement technologically, are already in demand among women in many less developed countries and are inexpensive. However, curbing population growth in this way can only lead to gradual changes in emissions and cannot be considered as a solution to the world's present pressing problem of rapidly rising temperatures which must be solved within the next few decades.

Although some population programmes are operated by the United Nations and the United States government it is also possible to contribute to charities that carry out similar work.

One such charity is Marie Stopes International which works closely with existing private healthcare providers, with governments, other aid agencies, academic institutions and non-governmental organisations in 37 countries. These countries include West Africa, a string of countries from Yemen to South Africa, Mexico, Bolivia and much of Asia. In 2014 the charity estimates that they prevented 5.4 million unintended pregnancies, 16,100 maternal deaths and 3.9 million unsafe abortions.[318] This appears to be a very effective charity to support if you have funds available from savings made by reducing your energy consumption.

Many other charities offer help with women's health education, girls' education, providing better water supplies, horticulture, microfinancing and similar projects often in specific less developed countries. These are all easy to find on the internet and some of them advertise through flyers that are inserted into magazines and similar publications. Such charities can provide very effective and satisfying ways of using donations from the general public, not always the better off, which can help directly and indirectly to limit population growth.

Summary

- *It is hard to judge objectively whether an energy saving project is worthwhile on financial grounds but be aware there is also a hidden cost involved in doing nothing to mitigate climate change.*

- *The rebound effect should always be avoided, or at least minimised, when spending any savings made from saving energy.*

- *Surprisingly the use of time has a carbon footprint depending on how that time is used.*

- *Savings made from using less energy may be spent on capital investment, including community renewable energy schemes, as well as on low-carbon activities.*

- *There are many charities, especially in developing countries, which are in need of funds to conduct environmentally positive actions.*

- *The growing global population threatens to exacerbate climate change. Help is needed to reduce population growth, including the support of charities that concentrate on improving the (reproductive) health and education of young women and girls.*

CHAPTER 11: DECISION TIME

"Once to every man and nation, comes the moment to decide,
In the strife of truth with falsehood, for the good or evil side;
Some great cause, some great decision, offering each the bloom or
blight,
And the choice goes by forever, 'twixt that darkness and that light."
Poem by James Russell Lowell, 1845[319]

My intention in writing this book is to encourage individuals and households, particularly the better off, to take greater responsibility for the emissions from their homes and lifestyles. It is a cop out for those of us who are better off to wait for government, whether local or national, to tell us what to do and even to pay for or subsidise what can be done at a personal level. The technical solutions to reducing carbon emissions are obvious but their implementation is held back by politics and by those with a vested interest in the *status quo*. Given the urgency with which climate change needs to be addressed the time for decisions and action is now.

Successive UK governments have failed to demonstrate leadership in mitigating climate change and have tended to hide behind the 'fig leaf' of the Climate Change Act (2008) and the UK's supposed adherence to the mandatory target of a reduction of 80 per cent in emissions relative to 1990 by 2050. As Lord Deben, Chairman of the Committee on Climate Change, stated in the Foreword to the Committee's 2016 report to parliament *"... current policies are insufficient to meet the requirements of the fourth and fifth carbon budgets and keep us on a cost-effective path to the 2050 target."*[320] Later in the full report the Committee notes that in the last three years reduction in emissions has come almost exclusively from changes in electricity generation. The annual rates of installing cavity wall and loft insulation in homes have fallen by 60 and 90 per cent, respectively, and less than 2.5 per cent of heat demand was met from low-carbon sources such as heat pumps and solar thermal panels. In the past year, emissions have been rising in the transport and agriculture sectors.

One problem is that the metric used by government to calculate the UK's emissions provides too much opportunity to omit some emissions from the calculations. The metric distinguishes between what are called non-traded and traded emissions. The non-traded emissions include those from the use of road transport, agriculture and buildings. Non-traded sector emissions accounted for 59% of total UK greenhouse gas emissions in 2012.[321] The traded emissions are based on the UK's share of the limit set by the European Union's Emissions Trading System (EU ETS) for each five-year carbon budgeting period and mostly cover power and heavy industry.[322] Companies in this sector have the option to buy and sell emissions permits across the EU.

Thus the law firm Client Earth has pointed out that, as the UK target excludes the true contribution to emissions from the power sector and heavy industry, "… *the UK will not be compelled by law to reduce its emissions there sufficiently fast. The 2013 Energy Act addressed this by putting in place a framework for a domestic carbon intensity target. This set out to ensure that emissions in the traded sector (measured per unit of electricity generated) decreased over set timescales. The current government has decided not to implement a carbon intensity target. In its absence, we continue to rely on the ETS to drive* [the UK's] *emissions reductions – and its ability to do so is far from certain.*"[323]

Lastly, the emissions metric neither takes complete account of emissions from international shipping and aviation nor does it include emissions embedded in imported goods. In effect the Act uses production emissions (emissions caused by the manufacture of goods within the UK) and not consumption emissions (including emissions attributable to imported goods caused by their manufacture overseas). Emissions from imports constituted 55 per cent of the greenhouse gas emissions associated with the UK's carbon footprint in 2013.[324]

Leaving the murky details of the Climate Change Act behind I hope that having read this far you will have realised that there is a lot that individuals, and especially better-off individuals, can do to reduce their personal carbon footprint. You can also influence others by setting an example, telling people (family, friends and neighbours) what you are doing and why. Not everyone will choose to make savings in the same way because our personal situations, priorities and lifestyles differ. The important thing for us as individuals is to pick ways in which we can cut our emissions, set targets that we will achieve and stick to them. This can be done individually or as a household. It is probably easier to work with others in your household so that you can support each other.

You can also work with others through local environmental groups such as those formed under the Transition Towns movement[325] and as part of Friends of the Earth and there are many other groups associated with national organisations which are mentioned in Chapter 10. One successful means of encouraging neighbours and work colleagues to come together to reduce their personal carbon footprint was started over 20 years ago by David Gershon of the Empowerment Institute in the USA. He devised a way to challenge small groups of a dozen or so to work together to cut their footprints and described this in the book *Low Carbon Diet: A 30 Day Program to Lose 5000 Pounds*.[326] The concept has been used in Australia and is now starting to gain a foothold in the UK under the name 'Cool Communities'.[327]

But you may wonder how individuals, or even small groups working together, can eventually have any effect on government or even on society in general. The key is to alter what sociologists call the norms of behaviour. *"Norms can be divided into two different types, one at the societal level (social norms), and one at the personal level (personal norms). Social norms that have been internalised and that gain strength from personal conscience rather than from what others may expect are referred to as personal norms. Personal norms reflect commitment to internalised values and are experienced as feelings of personal obligation to engage in certain behaviour and an ascription to a personal responsibility to take action. In order to internalise a social norm, a person needs to adopt it as a personal standard of conduct."*[328] This quotation makes it seem as though personal norms can only change under the influence of social norms but in some situations, such as mitigating climate change, I would expect the opposite to be true. I would expect that the personal convictions of a growing number of individuals and households will eventually, and maybe are already, leading to new social norms of behaviour.

I expect that we can all recall examples of how social norms have changed during our lifetimes. Think of lighting garden bonfires, smoking in public places, drink driving and not wearing seatbelts in cars, all of which now attract public opprobrium, and may even be illegal today. But on the whole these were changes that took time to be accepted and were brought about by changes in legislation even accompanied by extensive advertising. The problem with mitigating climate change is that time really is of the essence. As we've seen, humanity only has at most 20 years to solve the problem.

This may all seem too daunting. You may reasonably ask how society as a whole can be convinced to change by the actions of a small number of people. But the answer from previous experience is that only a relatively small proportion of people have to change their attitudes for a new social norm to become accepted.

192

Malcolm Gladwell in his book *The Tipping Point* has shown how *"little things can make a big difference"*.[329] In his book he quotes examples which he compares to the spread of a medical epidemic. At some level an infectious disease can exist within a population without affecting the majority but if that level exceeds a certain threshold, which Gladwell calls the tipping point, then the disease can become an epidemic and affect a very large part of, if not all, the population. Exactly at what level the tipping point kicks in depends on the situation but there is no doubt that many situations can pass through such a transformation or an almost explosive change and give rise to very rapid shifts in behaviour and outcomes. There is no reason that I know of why this could not happen with people's attitude to climate mitigation too.

But, as mentioned above, personal norms are important too. We have to accept responsibility for our actions. This is powerfully expressed by Rose Bridger at the end of her book *Plane Truth* in which she explores the mostly negative impacts of aviation on humanity and the natural world. She says that non-business passengers are eager to reap the benefits of flying because it enables them to take holidays in otherwise inaccessible places and to visit faraway family and friends. She continues *"This is only possible because* [the passengers] *pay little of the true cost, but I believe personal responsibility is also important, and that everyone who does fly has a duty to make a concerted effort to minimise the number of flights they take"*.[330] One might also add that everyone has a duty to give up flying, at least for purely leisure reasons, altogether.

We can see encouraging signs of positive change in some aspects of our daily lives yet many of us are continually frustrated at the slow rate of progress. Indeed, some of the current trends remain in the wrong direction and some forms of behaviour, such as driving a car that is far bigger or more powerful than is really needed, apparently simply to boost the owner's status, and flying abroad on holiday, appear sacrosanct. Similarly, as was pointed out in an Ipsos MORI report in 2007, "*As citizens* [people] *want to avert climate change but, at the same time, as consumers they want to go on holiday, own a second home, a big car and the latest electronic goods.*"[331] Those of us who can afford such luxuries, and that is all they are because the vast majority of people in the UK and elsewhere in the world live happily without them, must learn to cut back on such items and find other, less carbon intensive, ways to spend their money. It's a remarkable fact that only about one person in twenty of the world's population has ever flown and, not surprisingly, these people live mostly in industrialised countries.[332] Those of us who are better off and mostly living in developed countries can no longer have our cake and eat it as regards climate change as I hope I have explained.

It is also worth recalling that there is evidence to suggest that increasing affluence does not lead necessarily to more happiness and well-being. For example, the philosopher and journalist James Garvey, in his book *The Persuaders*, notes that "*... people with materialistic values are actually psychologically worse off than people who value other sorts of things. And materialism undermines not just individual happiness, but social cohesion as well*". He pursues this argument at some length without being able to demonstrate whether unhappiness causes the pursuit of money or *vice versa,* or whether there is a third factor at work, but the correlation between the two seems well established.[333]

The theme of personal responsibility was touched on by Pope Francis in his Encyclical letter *Laudato Si'* (Praise be to you) published in 2015.[334] He discusses climate change in the wider context of global poverty, the abuse of nature, the lack of a feeling of responsibility for our fellow citizens and the pursuit of consumerism. He states his conviction that "*... everything is interconnected, and that genuine care for our own lives and our*

194

relationships with nature is inseparable from fraternity, justice and faithfulness to others." He continues "The natural environment is a collective good, the patrimony of all humanity and the responsibility of everyone."

In a similar vein Bill McKibben, the environmentalist and co-founder of 350.org, in his book *The End of Nature*,[335] questions whether mankind's response to climate change will be one of defiance or humility. Will mankind continue 'defiantly' on its present path and try to solve the problem by the use of technology alone alongside increasing growth in the global economy and in energy demand, consumption and population? Or will mankind come to recognise with humility that *Homo sapiens* is just one species among many interdependent species on the Earth and that all nature, for example the rain forest, is of value for its own sake and not just for how it can be of benefit to humanity? Will we learn to make mental, and not just technological, adjustments to our way of life and start to exercise restraint, particularly in regards to growth?

Climate change is just one problem among many interconnected challenges that the world faces today but it is probably the most urgent.

One final thought is how our behaviour today will affect future generations and even our children and grandchildren. Given the current state of our changing climate is this a legacy that we want to leave behind for future generations? Would it not be better for us to work, individually and together, towards bequeathing a better world by making some positive impacts now? As the American Indian saying goes "We do not inherit the Earth from our ancestors; we borrow it from our children."

Summary

- *Now is the time for better-off individuals to decide how they will reduce their carbon footprints.*
- *Recent UK governments have consistently failed to match their actions to their words.*
- *There are ways to work with others and in local groups, as well as individually, to cut carbon emissions.*
- *The norms of behaviour in society can, and do, change and it is possible for active groups in society to bring about such changes.*
- *The better off are in a more advantageous position than most to initiate such changes.*
- *If we wish to bequeath a better world to our children and grandchildren we need to act now.*

ACKNOWLEDGEMENTS

I am indebted to many colleagues and friends with whom I have had discussions on saving energy and reducing emissions over at least the past decade. I owe a huge debt to Richard Genn, an inspirational teacher who first sparked my interest in environmental science, and to Robert Hutchison, whose leadership and clarity of objectives made the path easier.

For finding time to read early drafts of the book and for their very helpful comments and feedback I am very grateful to Brian Davey, Sam Espig, Lisa Jackson, James Martin-Jones, Brian Shorter, Andy Smale, Rob Veck, Peggy Vermeesch and Maya Whitmarsh.

All the householders I approached when preparing to write Chapter 9, for whom I have used pseudonyms, welcomed me into their homes and provided lots of useful information about retrofitting, constructing and living in a low-carbon house. I thank them for their help.

As always, any views expressed here and any mistakes or errors are mine alone and I welcome feedback at bobwhitmarsh566@talktalk.net.

INDEX

201

NOTES AND REFERENCES
(all web sites were accessed on 25 January 2017)

PREFACE

[1] This is an extreme interpretation of my carbon emissions. How to calculate emissions from electricity supplied by companies that include a proportion of low-carbon renewable energy is debatable as I'll explain in Chapter 4.

[2] I shall use the generally accepted shorthand that 'carbon emissions' actually refers to emissions of carbon dioxide and other greenhouse gases.

[3] See the cash savings ratio in Figure 4 at https://www.ons.gov.uk/peoplepopulationandcommunity/personalandhouseholdfinances/incomeandwealth/articles/alternativemeasuresofrealhouseholdsdisposableincomeandthesavingratio/dec2016

CHAPTER 1

[4] Hansen, James. "I am an Energy Voter," m.s. February 23, 2016. http://www.columbia.edu/~jeh1/. Hansen is a US climate scientist and former Director of the NASA Goddard Institute for Space Studies.

[5] If you would like to find more information there are many web sites that explain the scientific basis of climate change and its likely consequences in an objective way. See http://www.metoffice.gov.uk/climate-guide/climate-change; http://www.wwf.org.uk/what_we_do/tackling_climate_change/climate_change_explained/; https://www.theccc.org.uk/tackling-climate-change/the-science-of-climate-change/. A technical synthesis of the 2014 reports of the Intergovernmental Panel on Climate Change (IPCC), which includes a 24-page Summary for Policy Makers, can also be downloaded from http://ar5-syr.ipcc.ch/.

[6] Strictly as the atmosphere gets warmer it can hold slightly more water vapour. The amount doubles with every 10°C rise which is why global warming is accompanied by heavier rain fall.

[7] I shall use the chemical formula CO_2 for carbon dioxide from now on simply to save space.

[8] The rates of these processes on timescales of centuries is hard or impossible to measure because of the limited resolution of geological dating methods going back more than 4 million years but the rates of change in the global trends in temperature are estimated to be at least nine times slower than what is occurring today.

[9] Juniper, Tony, 'What nature does for Britain', pp.281, Profile Books.

[10] Hansen, James, Sato, Makiko, Ruedy, Reto, Schmidt, Gavin A., Lo, Ken, and Persin, Avi. "Global Temperature in 2016," m.s. January 18, 2017. http://www.columbia.edu/~jeh1/

[11] Zeebe, Richard E., Andy Ridgwell, and James C. Zachos. "Anthropogenic Carbon Release Rate Unprecedented during the Past 66 Million Years." Nature Geoscience, March 21, 2016.

[12] Allen, M.R., Barros, V.R., and many others. "Climate Change 2014 Synthesis Report: Approved Summary for Policymakers." Geneva: IPCC, November 1, 2014.

[13] http://edition.cnn.com/2016/02/20/us/tropical-cyclone-winston-fiji/

[14] http://www.eea.europa.eu/highlights/floodplain-management-reducing-flood-risks

[15] http://www.bom.gov.au/climate/drought/

[16] Schaller, Nathalie, Alison L. Kay, Rob Lamb, Neil R. Massey, Geert Jan van Oldenborgh, Friederike E. L. Otto, Sarah N. Sparrow, et al. "Human Influence on Climate in the 2014 Southern England Winter Floods and Their Impacts." Nature Climate Change, February 1, 2016.

[17] Carbon Brief Weekly Briefing, 14 January 2016.

[18] Ward, Robert, and Ranger, Nicola. "Trends in economic and insured losses from weather-related events: A New Analysis." Insurance Industry Brief. Munich Re and Centre for Climate Change Economics and Policy, November 2010. http://cccep.ac.uk/wp-content/uploads/2015/10/economic-trends-insured-losses.pdf.

[19] http://www.argo.ucsd.edu/global_change_analysis.html#temp

[20] Pachauri, Rajendra K., and Meyer, L.A. (eds.). "IPCC 2014: Climate Change 2014: Synthesis Report. Contribution of WGs I, II and III to the Fifth Assessment Report of the IPCC." Intergovernmental Panel on Climate Change (IPCC), 2014.

[21] Nicholls, R.J., N. Marinova, J.A. Lowe, S. Brown, P. Vellinga, D. de Gusmão, J. Hinkel, and R.S.J. Tol. "Sea-Level Rise and Its Possible

Impacts given a 'beyond 4°C World' in the Twenty-First Century." *Phil. Trans. R. Soc. Lond. A* 369, (2011): 161–81.

[22] de la Vega-Leinert, Anne C., and Robert J. Nicholls. "Potential Implications of Sea-Level Rise for Great Britain." *Journal of Coastal Research* 242 (March 2008): 342–57.

[23] http://www.ipcc.ch/ipccreports/tar/wg2/index.php?idp=671

[24] Albert, Simon, Javier X Leon, Alistair R Grinham, John A Church, Badin R Gibbes, and Colin D Woodroffe. "Interactions between Sea-Level Rise and Wave Exposure on Reef Island Dynamics in the Solomon Islands." *Environmental Research Letters* 11, no. 5 (May 1, 2016).

[25] Dutton, A., A. E. Carlson, A. J. Long, G. A. Milne, P. U. Clark, R. DeConto, B. P. Horton, S. Rahmstorf, and M. E. Raymo. "Sea-Level Rise due to Polar Ice-Sheet Mass Loss during Past Warm Periods." *Science* 349, no. 6244 (July 10, 2015).

[26] Srokosz, M. A., and H. L. Bryden. "Observing the Atlantic Meridional Overturning Circulation Yields a Decade of Inevitable Surprises." *Science* 348, no. 6241 (June 19, 2015).

[27] Hansen, James, and Sato, Makiko. "Predictions Implicit in 'Ice Melt' Paper and Global Implications," m.s., September 21, 2015. http://www.columbia.edu/~jeh1/

[28] Anon. "Subtle Signals at Sea." *Nature Geoscience* 9, no. 7 (June 29, 2016): 471–471.

[29] Costello, Anthony, Mustafa Abbas, Adriana Allen, Sarah Ball, Sarah Bell, Richard Bellamy, Sharon Friel, et al. "Managing the Health Effects of Climate Change." *The Lancet* 373, no. 9676 (May 2009): 1693–1733.

[30] Crimmins, Alison, Balbus, John, Gamble, Janet L., Beard, Charles B., Bell, Jesse E., and 11 others. "The Impacts of Climate Change on Human Health in the United States: A Scientific Assessment." Washington, D.C.: U.S. Global Change Research Program, 2016.

[31] http://www.floridahealth.gov/diseases-and-conditions/zika-virus/

[32] http://www.climate-change-guide.com/dengue-fever.html

[33] https://www.theguardian.com/world/2016/aug/01/anthrax-outbreak-climate-change-arctic-circle-russia

[34] Juniper, Tony. *What Has Nature Ever Done for Us?* Profile Books, 2013; *What Nature Does for Britain*. London, UK: Profile Books, 2015.

[35] http://www.ucsusa.org/global_warming/science_and_impacts/impacts/impacts-of-climate-on-coffee.html#.WIiCY01viUk

[36] Allen, M.R., Barros, V.R., and others. "Climate Change 2014 Synthesis Report: Approved Summary for Policymakers." Geneva: IPCC, November 1, 2014.

[37] Jezkova, Tereza, and John J. Wiens. "Rates of Change in Climatic Niches in Plant and Animal Populations Are Much Slower than Projected Climate Change." *Proceedings of the Royal Society B: Biological Sciences* 283, no. 1843 (November 30, 2016).

[38] McGuire, Jenny L., Joshua J. Lawler, Brad H. McRae, Tristan A. Nuñez, and David M. Theobald. "Achieving Climate Connectivity in a Fragmented Landscape." *Proceedings of the National Academy of Sciences* 113, no. 26 (June 28, 2016): 7195–7200.

[39] Thackeray, Stephen J., Peter A. Henrys, Deborah Hemming, James R. Bell, Marc S. Botham, Sarah Burthe, Pierre Helaouet, et al. "Phenological Sensitivity to Climate across Taxa and Trophic Levels." *Nature*, June 29, 2016.

[40] Visser, Marcel E. "Phenology: Interactions of Climate Change and Species." *Nature*, June 29, 2016.

[41] Anon. "Global Risks Report 2016: 11th Edition." Insight Report. World Economic Forum; Marsh & McLennan Companies; Zurich Insurance Group, no date.

[42] Hulme, M. *Why We Disagree About Climate Change: Understanding Controversy, Inaction and Opportunity*. Cambridge University Press, 2009.

[43] Carbon Brief, weekly briefing, 5 February 2016.

[44] http://biasedbbc.org/blog/2016/04/25/climate-change-change/

[45] Washington, H., and J. Cook. Climate *Change Denial: Heads in the Sand*. Earthscan, 2011.

[46] Doran, P.T., and M. Kendall Zimmerman. "Examining the Scientific Consensus on Climate Change." *EOS* 90, no. 3 (2009): 22–23.

[47] Anderegg, W.R.L., J.W. Prall, J. Harold, and S.H. Schneider. "Expert Credibility in Climate Change." *Proceedings of the National Academy of Sciences* 107, no. 27 (2010): 12107–9.

[48] Hornsey, Matthew J., Emily A. Harris, Paul G. Bain, and Kelly S. Fielding. "Meta-Analyses of the Determinants and Outcomes of Belief in Climate Change." *Nature Climate Change*, February 22, 2016.

[49] Many of Ajzen's publications on this topic are referenced at http://people.umass.edu/aizen/publications.html

[50] Hibbing, John R., Kevin B. Smith, and John R. Alford. "Differences in Negativity Bias Underlie Variations in Political Ideology." *Behavioral and Brain Sciences* 37, no. 3 (June 2014): 297–307.

[51] Shuckburgh, E., R. Robison, and N. Pidgeon. "Climate Science, the Public and the News Media: Summary Findings of a Survey and Focus Groups Conducted in the UK in March 2011." NERC (Living with Environmental Change programme), September 28, 2012.

[52] http://www.washingtonpost.com/sf/national/2015/11/29/carbon/

[53] Tollefson, Jeff. "Paris Climate Deal Strains Carbon Accountancy." *Nature* 529, no. 7587 (January 26, 2016): 450–51.

[54] Moss, R.H., J.E. Edmonds, K.A. Hibbard, M.R. Manning, S.K. Rose, D.P. van Vuuren, T.R. Carter, et al. "The next Generation of Scenarios for Climate Change Research and Assessment." *Nature* 463, no. 11 February 2010.

[55] Based on 515 billion tonnes of carbon emitted between 1870 and 2011. IPCC WG1 Technical Summary, Box TFE.8 and Figure 1, p.103-104, 2013. The decadal baseline of 1861-1880 was chosen by IPCC to illustrate long-term trends.

[56] This is a result based on the statistics of running numerous simulations each of which contains a degree of randomness in its outcome.

[57] Stocker, Thomas, Qin, Dahe, and 8 others (Editors). "Working Group I Contribution to the IPCC Fifth Assessment Report: Climate Change 2013: The Physical Science Basis: Summary for Policymakers, Technical Summary and FAQs." Cambridge, UK: IPCC, 2013.

[58] http://cdiac.ornl.gov/trends/emis/meth_reg.html

[59] Net zero emissions means reaching a state where carbon emissions, if any, are balanced or exceeded by the concurrent natural and man-made take up of CO_2 from the atmosphere.

[60] Anderson, Kevin. "Duality in Climate Science." *Nature Geoscience*, October 12, 2015, pp.2.

[61] Rogelj, Joeri, Gunnar Luderer, Robert C. Pietzcker, Elmar Kriegler, Michiel Schaeffer, Volker Krey, and Keywan Riahi. "Energy System Transformations for Limiting End-of-Century Warming to below 1.5 °C." *Nature Climate Change* 5, no. 6 (May 21, 2015): 519–27.

[62] This book was largely written before the Brexit referendum result in June 2016. The subsequent impact on topics discussed here remains uncertain (January 2017).

[63]Klein, Naomi. *This Changes Everything*. Allen Lane, 2014.

[64] http://www.usmayors.org/climateprotection/agreement.htm

[65] Hartman, Hattie. "Bristol: Europe's Green Capital." m.s. Bristol, UK, March 26, 2015.

[66] http://www.theecologist.org/green_green_living/home/807176/top_10_greenest_uk_cities.html

CHAPTER 2

[67] Anon. "World Energy Outlook 2015 Factsheets." Paris, France: International Energy Agency (IEA), November 11, 2015.

[68] https://www.wri.org/blog/2017/01/china%E2%80%99s-decline-coal-consumption-drives-global-slowdown-emissions

[69] http://www.nature.com/news/china-s-carbon-emissions-could-peak-sooner-than-forecast-1.19597

[70] https://www.iea.org/publications/freepublications/publication/CO$_2$EmissionsFromFuelCombustionHighlights2015.pdf

[71] International Energy Statistics from the US Energy Information Administration.

[72] Hubbert, M.K. "Nuclear Energy and the Fossil Fuels." San Antonio, Texas, USA: American Petroleum Institute, 1956.

[73] Ragnarsdottir, Kristin Vala, and Sverdrup, Harald U. "Limits to Growth Revisited." *Geoscientist*, October 2015.

[74] The International Energy Agency (IEA) does not hold this view. It suggests there are ample physical oil and liquid fuel resources for the foreseeable future. This view may be coloured by the recent rapid expansion of shale oil production in the USA. See https://www.iea.org/countries/membercountries/.

[75] https://www.ft.com/content/a623e1e8-b11a-11e4-831b-00144feab7de

[76] http://shalebubble.org/

[77] http://peakoilbarrel.com/what-is-peak-oil/

[78] Raugei, Marco, and Enrica Leccisi. "A Comprehensive Assessment of the Energy Performance of the Full Range of Electricity Generation Technologies Deployed in the United Kingdom." *Energy Policy* 90 (March 2016): 46–59. See Figure 2.

[79] The unit of a kilowatt.hour (kWh) is explained in detail later on page 67.

[80] http://ec.europa.eu/eurostat/statistics-explained/index.php/Energy_production_and_imports

[81] https://www.gov.uk/government/uploads/system/uploads/attachment_data/file/552059/Chapter_5_web.pdf, Table 5.9.

[82] https://www.gov.uk/government/uploads/system/uploads/attachment_data/file/541318/DUKES_2016_Press_Notice.pdf

[83] Britain's last deep coal mine at Kellingley in North Yorkshire was closed in December 2016.

[84] https://www.gov.uk/government/uploads/system/uploads/attachment_data/file/540900/Chapter_2_web.pdf. Table 2B.

[85] http://oilandgasuk.co.uk/wp-content/uploads/2015/09/Oil-Gas-UK-Economic-Report-2015-low-res.pdf

[86] https://www.ofgem.gov.uk/electricity/transmission-networks/electricity-interconnectors

[87] https://www.gov.uk/government/uploads/system/uploads/attachment_data/file/540909/Chapter_3_web.pdf

[88] http://www.cityam.com/234877/oil-prices-uk-oil-baron-warns-chancellor-george-osborne-that-the-north-sea-industry-is-on-the-brink-of-destruction

[89] https://www.gov.uk/government/uploads/system/uploads/attachment_data/file/540923/Chapter_4_web.pdf

[90] 'Reserves' means firm estimates of the quantity of a particular mineral in the ground; 'resources' are cruder estimates based on less information and are less reliable.

[91] McGlade, Christophe, and Paul Ekins. "The Geographical Distribution of Fossil Fuels Unused When Limiting Global Warming to 2 °C." *Nature* 517, no. 7533 (January 7, 2015): 187–90.

[92] Since I wrote this the think-tank Oil Change International has emphasised this conclusion in a 60-page report 'The Sky's Limit' published in September 2016. See http://priceofoil.org/2016/09/22/the-skys-limit-report/

[93] IPCC WG1. "The Physical Science Basis Chapter 8." IPCC AR5, 2013.

[94] Schneising, Oliver, John P. Burrows, Russell R. Dickerson, Michael Buchwitz, Maximilian Reuter, and Heinrich Bovensmann. "Remote Sensing of Fugitive Methane Emissions from Oil and Gas Production in North American Tight Geologic Formations: Remote Sensing of Fugitive

212

Methane Emissions from Oil and Gas Production." *Earth's Future* 2, no. 10 (October 2014): 548–58.

[95] Caulton, D. R., P. B. Shepson, R. L. Santoro, J. P. Sparks, R. W. Howarth, A. R. Ingraffea, M. O. L. Cambaliza, et al. "Toward a Better Understanding and Quantification of Methane Emissions from Shale Gas Development." *Proceedings of the National Academy of Sciences*, April 14, 2014.

[96] Karion, A., and 18 others. "Methane Emissions Estimate from Airborne Measurements over a Western United States Natural Gas Field." *Geophysical Research Letters* 40, no. 16 (2013): 4393–97.

[97] Alvarez, R.A., S.W. Pacala, J.J. Winebrake, W.L. Chameides, and S.P. Hamburg. "Greater Focus Needed on Methane Leakage from Natural Gas Infrastructure." *Proceedings of the National Academy of Sciences*, April 24, 2012. 109, no. 17, 6435-6440.

[98] Andrews, I.J. "The Jurassic Shales of the Weald Basin: Geology and Shale Oil and Shale Gas Resource Estimation." London, UK: BGS/DECC, May 23, 2014.

[99] Fracking is banned in Scotland and Wales.

[100] https://www.foe.co.uk/sites/default/files/downloads/government-backtracks-fracking-safeguards-drinking-water-protected-areas-81601.pdf; https://www.foe.co.uk/sites/default/files/downloads/facts-about-fracking-85615.pdf

[101] http://ieefa.org/world-passes-peak-coal-as-global-consumption-declines/

[102] https://www.iea.org/publications/freepublications/publication/CO$_2$EmissionsFromFuelCombustionHighlights2015.pdf

[103] Zhu, Qian. "High-Efficiency Power Generation – Review of Alternative Systems." Report 247, IEA Clean Coal Centre, March 2015. Pp.120.

[104] Nalbandian, Hermine. "Climate Implications of Coal-to-Gas Substitution in Power Generation." London, UK: IEA Clean Coal Centre, April 2015.

[105] https://www.gov.uk/government/statistics/electricity-chapter-5-digest-of-united-kingdom-energy-statistics-dukes, Table 5.9.

[106] http://www.carbonbrief.org/iea-un-pledges-will-cause-dramatic-slowdown-in-energy-emissions-by-2030; Fig.2.

[107] http://ipcc.ch/pdf/assessment-report/ar5/wg3/ipcc_wg3_ar5_chapter10.pdf, Figure 10.1.

[108] Cook, P.J. *Clean Energy, Climate and Carbon*. CRC Press, 2012.

[109] A cap rock is a rock layer that is relatively impermeable and acts as a natural seal preventing the upward migration of fluids or gas.

[110] Arts, Rob, Eiken, Ola, Chadwick, Andy, Zweigel, Peter, van de Meer, Bert, and Kirby, Gary. "Seismic Monitoring at the Sleipner Underground CO_2 Storage Site (North Sea)." In *Geological Storage of Carbon Dioxide*, 181–191. Geological Society Special Publication 233. London, UK, 2004.

[111] http://www.bgs.ac.uk/science/CO_2/home.html

[112] Anon. "The Global Status of CCS: 2015 Summary Report." Global CCS Institute, 2015. http://hub.globalccsinstitute.com/sites/default/files/publications/196843/global-status-ccs-2015-summary.pdf.

[113] http://www.nature.com/news/no-magic-fix-for-carbon-1.15118

[114] Cressey, Daniel. "Commercial Boost for Firms That Suck Carbon from Air." *Nature* 526, no. 7573 (October 14, 2015): 306–7.

[115] http://www.who.int/mediacentre/news/releases/2016/air-pollution-estimates/en/

[116] https://www.rcplondon.ac.uk/projects/outputs/every-breath-we-take-lifelong-impact-air-pollution

[117] http://www.imo.org/en/OurWork/Environment/PollutionPrevention/Pages/Default.aspx

[118] http://www.restud.com/wp-content/uploads/2015/09/MS17397manuscript.pdf

[119] http://www.edf.org/sites/default/files/AWMA-EM-airPollutionFromOilAndGas.pdf

[120] Petron, Gabrielle. "Air Pollution Issues Associated with Shale Gas Production" *The Bridge*, Summer 2014.

[121] https://www.french-property.com/guides/france/utilities/electricity/tariff/

[122] Fleming, D. (2007). "The lean guide to nuclear energy: A life-cycle in trouble". London, The Lean Economy Connection; Lenzen, M. (2008). "Life cycle energy and greenhouse gas emissions of nuclear energy: A review." *Energy Conversion and Management* 49: 2178-2199.

[123] As reported in Table 4 of Mez, L. (2012). "Nuclear energy–Any solution for sustainability and climate protection?" *Energy Policy* 48: 56-63.

[124] http://www.bbc.co.uk/news/business-35583740

[125] http://www.researchresearch.com/index.php?option=com_news&template=rr_2col&view=article&articleId=1337882

[126] Anon. "Engineering the UK electricity gap." London: Institution of Mechanical Engineers, 2016.

[127] https://en.wikipedia.org/wiki/Flamanville_Nuclear_Power_Plant

[128] https://en.wikipedia.org/wiki/Olkiluoto_Nuclear_Power_Plant

[129] http://www.world-nuclear.org/information-library/nuclear-fuel-cycle/nuclear-power-reactors/small-nuclear-power-reactors.aspx

[130] Anon. "Future Energy Scenarios in 5 Minutes," July 2016, National Grid

[131] Smith Stegen, Karen. "Heavy Rare Earths, Permanent Magnets, and Renewable Energies: An Imminent Crisis." *Energy Policy* 79 (April 2015): 1–8.

[132] Hertwich, E. G., T. Gibon, E. A. Bouman, A. Arvesen, S. Suh, G. A. Heath, J. D. Bergesen, A. Ramirez, M. I. Vega, and L. Shi. "Integrated Life-Cycle Assessment of Electricity-Supply Scenarios Confirms Global Environmental Benefit of Low-Carbon Technologies." *Proceedings of the National Academy of Sciences*, October 6, 2014. See Figure 1 in particular.

[133] Carbon Brief Weekly Briefing, 8 October 2015.

[134] http://ec.europa.eu/eurostat/statistics-explained/index.php/Renewable_energy_statistics#Electricity

[135] https://www.gov.uk/government/uploads/system/uploads/attachment_data/file/547977/Chapter_6_web.pdf

[136] *MacKay, D.J.C. Sustainable Energy - without the Hot Air. Cambridge: UIT, 2008.* Fig.28.2 and Table 28.3. David Mackay maintained these arguments in an interview in May 2016 only days before his death [http://www.theguardian.com/environment/2016/may/03/idea-of-renewables-powering-uk-is-an-appalling-delusion-david-mackay].

[137] Anon. "Who's Getting Ready for Zero?" CAT and TRACK, no date. http://zerocarbonbritain.org/images/pdfs/WGRZ%20exec%20sum.pdf.

[138] Jacobson, Mark. "100% Wind, Water, and Solar (WWS) All-Sector Energy Roadmaps for Countries and States," December 2015.

http://web.stanford.edu/group/efmh/jacobson/Articles/I/WWS-50-USState-plans.html.

[139] Allen, Paul, Yamin, Farhana, Bottoms, Isabel, and James, Phillip. "Who's getting ready for zero? Zero Britain Carbon: A Report on the State of Play of Zero Carbon Modelling." Machynlleth: Centre for Alternative Energy and TRACK, 2015; Allen, P., L. Blake, P. Harper, A. Hooker-Stroud, P. James, and T. Kellner. *Zero Carbon Britain: Rethinking the Future*. Machynlleth: CAT, 2013; Anon. "Options, Choices, Actions: UK Scenarios for a Low Carbon Energy System Transition." Loughborough: Energy Technologies Institute, 2015; Kahya, Damian. "4 Ways the UK Can Get Almost All Its Power from Renewables – without Hinkley." *Greenpeace Energy Desk*, September 21, 2015. http://energydesk.greenpeace.org/2015/09/21/4-ways-the-uk-can-get-almost-all-its-power-from-renewables/.

CHAPTER 3

[140] Boden, T.A., G. Marland, and R.J. Andres. 2011. Global, Regional, and National Fossil-Fuel CO_2 Emissions. Carbon Dioxide Information Analysis Center, Oak Ridge National Laboratory, U.S. Department of Energy, Oak Ridge, Tenn., U.S.A.

[141] http://www.mirror.co.uk/news/uk-news/uk-among-worst-offenders-comes-6944249

[142] Hansen, James. "Statement of Witness James E. Hansen." m.s. undated. http://www.columbia.edu/~jeh1/

[143] Direct emissions come from easily measureable consumptions of energy (electricity, gas and car fuel); indirect emissions come from the manufacture and supply of goods and provision of services.

[144] Anon. "Extreme carbon inequality: Why the Paris Climate Deal Must Put the Poorest, Lowest Emitting and Most Vulnerable People First." Oxfam Media Briefing. Oxfam, December 2, 2015.

[145] Usually emissions are also greater in countries with larger gross domestic products (GDPs) but I avoid getting into economics and restrict myself to discussing the behaviour of individuals.

[146] Chancel, Lucas, and Piketty, Thomas. "Carbon and Inequality: From Kyoto to Paris Trends in the Global Inequality of Carbon Emissions (1998-2013) & Prospects for an Equitable Adaptation Fund." Paris, France: Paris School of Economics, November 3, 2015.

216

[147] Wiedenhofer, Dominik, Dabo Guan, Zhu Liu, Jing Meng, Ning Zhang, and Yi-Ming Wei. "Unequal Household Carbon Footprints in China." *Nature Climate Change* 7, no. 1 (December 19, 2016): 75–80.

[148] S. Hallegatte et al. 'Shock Waves: Managing the impacts of climate change on Poverty, https://openknowledge.worldbank.org/bitstream/handle/10986/22787/9781464806735.pdf

[149] 'Rising Seas Disproportionately Threaten Gulf's Poorest', http://assets.climatecentral.org/pdfs/SLR-PressRelease-LA-MS-AL.pdf

[150] Ian Black at http://www.theguardian.com/world/2016/jan/22/austerity-saudi-style-cheap-oil-nudges-riyadh-toward-economic-reform

[151] BRICS is shorthand for Brazil, Russia, India, China and South Africa

[152] This refers to a special index, called the Theil index, used by economists Lucas Chancel and Thomas Piketty in their paper "Carbon and Inequality: From Kyoto to Paris Trends in the Global Inequality of Carbon Emissions (1998-2013) & Prospects for an Equitable Adaptation Fund." Paris, France: Paris School of Economics, November 3, 2015.

[153] 50% of 49% is 24.5% but since individual emissions are estimated to account for 64% of all global emissions 64% of 24.5% is 16%.

[154] This excludes 703,000 households in Northern Ireland which make up 2.66% of all UK households (UK Census 2011).

[155] Anon. "Government-Backed Energy Efficiency Measures Installed in Homes Plummet by 80 per Cent since 2012." *Energy in Buildings & Industry*, 2016. Article based on a report from the Association for the Conservation of Energy.

[156] https://www.gov.uk/government/speeches/amber-rudds-speech-on-a-new-direction-for-uk-energy-policy

[157] Letter from Lord Bourne, Parliamentary Under Secretary of State for Energy and Climate Change to my MP, 27 January 2016.

[158] Hargreaves, Katy, Preston, Ian, White, Vicky, and Thumin, Joshua. "The distribution of household CO_2 emissions in Great Britain." Joseph Rowntree Foundation (Centre for Sustainable Energy and Environmental Change Institute, University of Oxford), March 2013.

[159] The report by Hargreaves et al. (2013) gives more details about the surveys. It appears that when calculating emissions from aircraft the

Civil Aviation Authority uses the government recommended multiplier of 1.9 to account for the warming effect of contrails and non-CO_2 gases.

[160] E.g. http://www.thecarbonaccount.com/carbonexplained/

[161] Berners-Lee, M. *How Bad Are Bananas? The Carbon Footprint of Everything*. London: Profile Books, 2010.

[162] This factor is simply the emissions of the richest 10% divided by the emissions of the poorest 10%.

[163] Brand, Christian, and Brenda Boardman. "Taming of the few—The Unequal Distribution of Greenhouse Gas Emissions from Personal Travel in the UK." *Energy Policy* 36, no. 1 (January 2008): 224–38. Figure 2. Air travel emissions in this paper were overestimated by a factor of 3/1.9 (about 58%) compared to current UK government practice.

[164] Because they used the relatively high multiplier of 3 times CO_2 emissions to estimate the total global warming from flights this figure becomes 12.1 tonnes CO_2 if the currently recommended multiplier of 1.9 is used.

[165] Anon. "Extreme carbon inequality: Why the Paris Climate Deal Must Put the Poorest, Lowest Emitting and Most Vulnerable People First." Oxfam Media Briefing. Oxfam, December 2, 2015.

[166] Buchs, Milena, and Schnepf, Sylke V. "UK Households' Carbon Footprint: A Comparison of the Association between Household Characteristics and Emissions from Home Energy, Transport and Other Goods and Services." IZA Discussion Paper. University of Southampton, 2013 quote a range of 513 to 527 Mt CO_2 in 2006-2009 for average household emissions and https://www.gov.uk/government/statistics/uks-carbon-footprint gives total UK consumption emissions of 887.7 and 816.7 Mt CO_2 for 2007 and 2008.

[167] An independent estimate of CO_2 emissions in Winchester District for 2011 gives a figure of about 46% for direct emissions from household electricity, gas, other fuels and private cars but excluding emissions from flying. Thus a national household figure of 61% of all emissions does not seem implausible. Source: unpublished reports by the author.

[168] Dietz, T., G.T. Gardner, J. Gilligan, P.C. Stern, and M.P. Vandenbergh. "Household Actions Can Provide a Behavioral Wedge to Rapidly Reduce US Carbon Emissions." *Proceedings of the National Academy of Sciences* 106, no. 44 (2009): 18452–56.

[169] Hargreaves, Katy, Preston, Ian, White, Vicky, and Thumin, Joshua. "The distribution of household CO_2 emissions in Great Britain." Joseph Rowntree Foundation (Centre for Sustainable Energy and Environmental Change Institute, University of Oxford), March 2013, Table 5.

[170] UK reconciliation data from https://www.gov.uk/government/statistics/uk-local-authority-and-regional-carbon-dioxide-emissions-national-statistics-2005-2013.

CHAPTER 4

[171] Electricity and gas meters come in different models. Some are digital and easy to read but older ones are analogue and have a row of rotating dials that alternately rotate clockwise and anticlockwise along the row. These need to be read with care. Energy companies provide assistance with reading meters either online or by free helpline phone numbers which should be printed on your bill.

[172] Go to https://www.citizensadvice.org.uk/consumer/energy/energy-supply/your-energy-meter/move-your-gas-or-electricity-meter/ for advice.

[173] http://www.gridcarbon.uk/ and http://www.reuk.co.uk/Real-Time-Carbon-Website.htm

[174] http://www.realtimecarbon.org/ and http://www.reuk.co.uk/Real-Time-Carbon-Website.htm

[175] Even if you have PV panels on the roof they won't be generating electricity at night and so I assume all the electricity will be coming from power stations on the national grid ignoring any electricity that you may generate by wind turbines or other renewable sources.

[176] The use of smart meters is contentious because of concerns around the possibly malign influence of their microwave radiation on human health. See https://www.emfscientist.org/index.php/science-policy/expert-emf-scientist-quotations. Smart meters rely on continuous radio-frequency transmissions in the home to link individual energy meters to a display. This is similar to the operation of Wi-Fi, mobile phones and some other appliances.

[177] https://www.gov.uk/guidance/smart-meters-how-they-work

[178] https://www.gov.uk/government/collections/government-conversion-factors-for-company-reporting comparing figures for LPG and burning oil (net CV).

[179] http://www.cplindustries.co.uk/cpl-industries-environmental-policy

[180] https://www.gov.uk/government/publications/greenhouse-gas-reporting-conversion-factors-2016

[181] Data for 2012 from https://www.gov.uk/government/collections/government-conversion-factors-for-company-reporting and http://www.ccwater.org.uk/savewaterandmoney/averagewateruse/

[182] CO_2e means the amount of CO_2 that would have the same effect on global warming as all the greenhouse gases that were emitted including CO_2. It is usually expressed as kilograms or tonnes of carbon dioxide equivalent.

[183] http://www.unitedutilities.com/documents/amr-leaflet.pdf

[184] The cheat involved software and defeat devices which recognised when the diesel vehicle was being tested and reduced emissions accordingly. Subsequently the UK Department for Transport conducted tests on a wide range of diesel vehicles from other manufacturers and found that on average test track driving caused 4.5 to 5 times more NOx and particulate emissions, depending on the engine type, than were measured in the standard laboratory test (https://www.gov.uk/government/publications/vehicle-emissions-testing-programme-conclusions). However NO_x emissions, while important, contribute to health problems rather than any significant increase in global warming.

[185] https://en.wikipedia.org/wiki/New_European_Driving_Cycle

[186] Page 23, para.52 in Defra/DECC (2011). 2011 Guidelines to Defra / DECC's GHG Conversion Factors for Company Reporting: Methodology paper for emissions factors. London, Defra/DECC: pp.102.

[187] Anonymous. "Quantifying the Impact of Real-World Driving on Total CO_2 Emissions from UK Cars and Vans." London: Committee on Climate Change, September 2015

[188] http://www.c2es.org/docUploads/aviation-and-marine-report-2009.pdf, Table 1. http://www.atag.org/facts-and-figures.html

[189] If you travel on business it makes sense to also try and reduce your business flights in order to minimise your emissions. Meetings can very easily be held over Skype or other types of video-conference calls nowadays so there is much less need to fly to meetings.

[190] Since 2005 in the UK the ratio has varied between 2.9 and 2.4 and has decrease markedly since 2012 as coal-burning power stations have been closed.

[191] http://www.carbonindependent.org/sources_basics.html

[192] 1050 million tonnes $CO2_e$ divided by a population of 64.1 million. See https://www.gov.uk/government/uploads/system/uploads/attachment _data/file/542558/Consumption_emissions_May16_Final.pdf and http://www.ons.gov.uk/peoplepopulationandcommunity/populationan dmigration/populationestimates/bulletins/annualmidyearpopulationes timates/2014-06-26

[193] IPCC WG1. "The Physical Science Basis Chapter 8." IPCC AR5, 2013, Table 8.7.

[194] https://www.gov.uk/government/collections/government-conversion-factors-for-company-reporting

[195] The UK's Department of Energy and Climate Change was replaced by the Department for Business, Energy and Industrial Strategy in July 2016.

[196] In fact if your electricity supplier provides 100% renewable energy then effectively emissions from this source should be zero except for losses in transmission and distribution. In 2015 DECC estimated these to be 0.03816 kg CO_2e/kWh or 38 kg per 1000 kWh.

[197] Excepting the effect of learning to ecodrive, annual mileage alone will also be a very good indicator of your emissions from a given car. Obviously, if you change cars then you will need to calculate emissions in kg CO_2e.

[198] Details of the calculation method are given at https://www.atmosfair.de/portal/documents/10184/20102/Document ation_Calculator_EN_2008.pdf/21655b2c-d943-4f87-a1b5-ff8607542cda.

[199] This approach assumes that the factor applies to the whole flight but strictly, as recognised by atmosfair, it is only true for the high-altitude cruising section. The assumption will involve minimal error for a long-

haul flight since proportionally the time spent climbing to and descending from the cruise altitude is relatively short.

[200] Jones, Rory V., and Kevin J. Lomas. "Determinants of High Electrical Energy Demand in UK Homes: Socio-Economic and Dwelling Characteristics." *Energy and Buildings* 101 (August 2015): 24–34.

[201] http://blog.caranddriver.com/why-your-trip-computer-isnt-giving-accurate-mpg-readings-and-how-to-fix-it/

[202] The text in this section, which was originally written by the author, has been largely taken from http://www.winacc.org.uk/faq/climate-science/setting-good-idea-and-what-offsetting-anyway.

[203] More details are available from http://www.parliament.uk/documents/post/postpn290.pdf.

CHAPTER 5

[204] Berners-Lee, M. *How Bad Are Bananas? The Carbon Footprint of Everything.* London: Profile Books, 2010.

[205] http://www.wrap.org.uk/about-us/about/wrap-and-circular-economy

CHAPTER 6

[206] The electricity conversion factor can be found at https://www.gov.uk/government/collections/government-conversion-factors-for-company-reporting. Download the file for yyyy, the year of interest, choose 'Conversion factors yyyy - Condensed set (for most users)' and then click on the 'UK electricity' tab in the downloaded spreadsheet. Click on the adjacent 'Transmissions and distribution' tab to obtain the conversion factor for losses incurred in transmission over the national grid.

[207] http://alexnld.com/product/electric-wall-switch-and-socket-eu-us-plug-socket-with-2-switches/

[208] For example see http://www.beko.co.uk/lifestyle/ecosmart

[209] http://www.whitegoodshelp.co.uk/can-you-connect-a-dishwasher-to-the-hot-water-supply/

[210] http://www.which.co.uk/news/2015/11/can-you-wash-up-in-cold-water-washing-up-myths-busted-423969/

[211] http://www.which.co.uk/reviews/tumble-dryers/article/gas-and-heat-pump-tumble-dryers

[212] http://www.ethicalconsumer.org/buyersguides/appliances/cookers.aspx

[213] Berners-Lee, M. *How Bad Are Bananas? The Carbon Footprint of Everything*. London: Profile Books, 2010, p.35.

[214] http://www.uswitch.com/energy-saving/guides/energy-efficient-cooking/

[215] http://www.whitegoodshelp.co.uk/all-white-goods-articles/

[216] http://www.confusedaboutenergy.co.uk/index.php/buying-household-appliances/85-cookers/118-cookers#.V392xMtTGUk

[217] http://www.green-shopping.co.uk/mr-d-s-thermal-cooker-and-cookbook.html

[218] http://www.yougen.co.uk/blog-entry/1948/Is+domestic+voltage+optimisation+all+it'27s+cracked+up+to+be'3F/

[219] http://www.meetmaslow.com/

CHAPTER 7

[220] http://www.ukace.org/wp-content/uploads/2013/03/ACE-and-EBR-fact-file-2013-03-Cold-man-of-Europe.pdf

[221] Egger, Christiane, Priewasser, Reinhold, Rumpl, Johanna, and Gignac, Magan. "Survey report 2015. Progress in Energy Efficiency Policies in the EU Member States - the Experts Perspective." Linz, Austria: Energy Efficiency Watch Project, 2015.

[222] Palmer, Jason, Godoy-Shimizu, Daniel, Tillson, Amy, and Mawditt, Ian. "Building Performance Evaluation Programme: Findings from Domestic Projects Making Reality Match Design." InnovateUK, January 2016.

[223] http://www.carbonbrief.org/explainer-europes-struggle-to-switch-on-low-carbon-heating

[224] https://www.gov.uk/government/uploads/system/uploads/attachment_data/file/345141/uk_housing_fact_file_2013.pdf, Table 3a.

[225] https://www.gov.uk/government/uploads/system/uploads/attachment_data/file/345141/uk_housing_fact_file_2013.pdf

[226] http://www.energysavingtrust.org.uk/domestic/electric-heating-systems

[227] 10 litres heated from 10 to 60°C requires 5×10^5 calories. Using a 91% efficient gas boiler this is equivalent to 0.5815/0.91 kWh. The conversion rate for gas is 0.18445 kg CO_2e/kWh.

223

[228] http://www.energysavingtrust.org.uk/domestic/home-insulation

[229] https://www.gov.uk/government/statistics/household-energy-efficiency-national-statistics-detailed-report-2015; Table 4.2.

[230] http://www.npl.co.uk/news/squashed-loft-insulation-50-per-cent-less-effective

[231] http://info.cat.org.uk/questions/heatpumps/do-i-need-lot-land-space-ground-source-heat-pump-gshp

[232]http://www.eauc.org.uk/academics_to_trial_green_energy_system_that_cou; http://www.caplinhomes.co.uk/technology/

CHAPTER 8

[233] Brand, Christian, and Brenda Boardman. "Taming of the few—The Unequal Distribution of Greenhouse Gas Emissions from Personal Travel in the UK." *Energy Policy* 36, no. 1 (January 2008): 224–38.

[234]https://www.gov.uk/government/uploads/system/uploads/attachment_data/file/457752/nts2014-01.pdf

[235] https://www.gov.uk/government/statistics/national-travel-survey-2014

[236] https://www.gov.uk/government/collections/government-conversion-factors-for-company-reporting

[237] A passenger.kilometre is a unit of one passenger travelling one kilometre.

[238] http://www.nhs.uk/Livewell/fitness/Pages/physical-activity-guidelines-for-adults.aspx

[239] https://liftshare.com/uk

[240] https://www.enterprisecarclub.co.uk/

[241]http://www.parkers.co.uk/cars/advice/buying/2013/september/automatic-versus-manual/

[242] http://www.nextgreencar.com/hybrid-cars/environmental-benefits/

[243] http://www.bikehub.co.uk/featured-articles/carrying-children-on-bikes/

[244] http://www.theaa.com/motoring_advice/fuels-and-environment/drive-smart.html

[245]Oehlschlaeger, Matthew A., Haowei Wang, and Mitra N. Sexton. "Prospects for Biofuels: A Review." *Journal of Thermal Science and Engineering Applications* 5, no. 2 (May 17, 2013): 021006.

[246] Wetzstein, M., and H. Wetzstein. "Four Myths Surrounding U.S. Biofuels." *Energy Policy* 39 (2011): 4308–12.

[247] https://en.wikipedia.org/wiki/Environmental_impact_of_aviation

[248] https://www.atmosfair.de/en/emissionsrechner

[249] https://www.gov.uk/government/uploads/system/uploads/attachment_data/file/553488/2016_methodology_paper_Final_V01-00.pdf

[250] Bows-Larkin, Alice. *Heathrow 13: Prof Alice Bows-Larkin's Expert Evidence on Aviation and Climate Change*, m.s. 2016.

[251] www.atmosfair.de/en

[252] https://www.gov.uk/government/uploads/system/uploads/attachment_data/file/336702/experiences-of-attitudes-towards-air-travel.pdf

[253] http://www.airportwatch.org.uk/2015/06/levy-on-frequent-leisure-flyers-proposed-to-make-airport-expansion-unnecessary/

[254] http://www.airportwatch.org.uk/the-problems/#keyfacts

[255] Anon. "Quantifying the Impact of Real-World Driving on Total CO_2 Emissions from UK Cars and Vans." London: Committee on Climate Change, September 2015.

[256] http://www.racfoundation.org/motoring-faqs/environment#a5

[257] http://www.rac.co.uk/route-planner/mileage-calculator/

[258] http://www.eurail.com/europe-by-train/high-speed-trains

[259] http://www.railway-technology.com/features/feature-the-10-fastest-high-speed-trains-in-europe/

[260] http://www.seat61.com/CO_2flights.htm#.Vvu0Pcv2aJA

[261] Anon. "Air and Rail: Setting the Record Straight (Environment, Investment, Mobility and Political Bias)." European Regions Airline Association, 2012.

[262] Kemp, Roger. "Take the Car and Save the Planet?" *IEE Power Engineer*, November 2004, 12–17.

[263] Unfortunately rail services, other than Eurostar, which start in the UK are no longer accounted for on this web site. Hopefully this situation will be resolved soon (January 2017).

[264] https://en.wikipedia.org/wiki/List_of_the_world%27s_largest_cruise_ships

[265] https://en.wikipedia.org/wiki/Environmental_impact_of_shipping

[266] http://www.statista.com/statistics/266274/passengers-of-cruise-operator-carnival-corporation-und-plc/ and Assurance Statement related to Greenhouse Gas Emissions Inventory and Greenhouse Gas

Emissions Assertion for Fiscal Year 2013 prepared for Carnival Corporation & plc by Lloyd's Register.

[267] Farreny, Ramon, Jordi Oliver-Solà, Machiel Lamers, Bas Amelung, Xavier Gabarrell, Joan Rieradevall, Martí Boada, and Javier Benayas. "Carbon Dioxide Emissions of Antarctic Tourism." *Antarctic Science* 23, no. 6 (December 2011): 556–66.

[268] http://www.cgdev.org/page/mapping-impacts-climate-change

[269] Althor, Glenn, James E. M. Watson, and Richard A. Fuller. "Global Mismatch between Greenhouse Gas Emissions and the Burden of Climate Change." *Scientific Reports* 6 (February 5, 2016): 20281.

[270] http://www.eurotunnelgroup.com/uploadedFiles/assets-uk/Shareholders-Investors/Publication/CSR-Reports/2014CSR-UK-EurotunnelGroup.pdf

[271] http://www.ecofriendlytourist.com/index.php/site-map/transport-no-fly-zone/uk-ferries/. The same figure of 0.12 kg CO_2e/km is quoted by https://en.wikipedia.org/wiki/Ferry#Europe.

[272] Based on a car weighing 2 tonnes with a load of 400 kg and figures supplied by P&O Ferrymasters at http://www.poferrymasters.com/about-us/the-environment/CO_2-emission-calculator

[273] https://en.wikipedia.org/wiki/Aviation_biofuel

[274] http://www.safug.org/case-studies/

CHAPTER 9

[275] http://www.legislation.gov.uk/uksi/2015/962/pdfs/uksiem_20150962_en.pdf

[276] Warren, Andrew. "Landlords Must Not Use This Loophole." *Energy in Buildings & Industry*, p. 12, 2016.

[277] https://www.gov.uk/topic/planning-development/building-regulations

[278] http://www.planningportal.gov.uk/permission/

[279] https://www.architecture.com/files/ribaholdings/policyandinternationalrelations/policy/environment/2principles_lc_design_refurb.pdf

[280] Data from http://www.winchesterweather.org.uk/

[281] Composite here means having several components which contribute to strength, durability and thermal insulation.

[282] Green Building Bible: volumes 1 and 2, Editor Keith Hall, Green Building Press.

[283] https://en.wikipedia.org/wiki/Brick#Middle_East_and_South_Asia

[284] S.Taylor, 2010. Offsite Production in the UK Construction Industry: A Brief Overview. Health and Safety Executive, 30 pages.

[285] Christophers, John, 2016. The zero carbon retrofit, *Clean Slate*, No.100, Summer 2016, Centre for Alternative Technology.

[286] https://www.gov.uk/government/publications/conservation-of-fuel-and-power-approved-document-l

[287] This unit refers to the cubic metres of air leaking through a square metre of wall per hour.

[288] http://www.passivhaus.org.uk/standard.jsp?id=122

[289] http://www.passivhaustrust.org.uk/what_is_passivhaus.php

[290] http://www.passivehouse-international.org/index.php?page_id=176

[291] Khan, Sabena, and Wilkes, Emily. "Energy Consumption in the UK (2014) Chapter 3: Domestic Energy Consumption in the UK between 1970 and 2013." London, UK: DECC, July 31, 2014.

[292] Cotterell, Janet, and Dadby, Adam. *The Passivhaus Handbook: A Practical Guide to Constructing and Retrofitting Buildings for Ultra-Low Energy Performance (Sustainable Building).* UIT Cambridge Ltd., 2012.

[293] http://www.passivhaustrust.org.uk/

[294] http://www.greenbuildingstore.co.uk/

[295] https://www.gov.uk/government/uploads/system/uploads/attachment_data/file/240190/statistical_release_estimates_home_insulation_levels_gb_july_13.pdf

[296] https://www.connaissancedesenergies.org/sites/default/files/pdf-actualites/ecuk_chapter_3_-_domestic_factsheet.pdf, Chart 5.

[297] Jones, Rory V., and Kevin J. Lomas. "Determinants of High Electrical Energy Demand in UK Homes: Appliance Ownership and Use." *Energy and Buildings* 117 (April 2016): 71–82.

CHAPTER 10

[298] Stern, Nicholas. "Economics: Current Climate Models Are Grossly Misleading." *Nature* 530, no. 7591 (February 24, 2016): 407–9.

[299] Crompton, T. "Common Cause: The Case for Working with Our Cultural Values." WWF UK, September 2010.

[300] As calculated by www.atmosfair.de/en but multiplied by a factor of 0.63 as described in Chapter 4 to correct for a multiplication factor of 1.9 instead of 3.

[301] http://www.dell.com/learn/us/en/vn/corp-comm/environment_carbon_footprint_products

[302] Berners-Lee, M. *How Bad Are Bananas? The Carbon Footprint of Everything*. London: Profile Books, 2010.

[303] Chitnis, Mona, Steve Sorrell, Angela Druckman, Steven K. Firth, and Tim Jackson. "Turning Lights into Flights: Estimating Direct and Indirect Rebound Effects for UK Households." *Energy Policy, Special Section: Long Run Transitions to Sustainable Economic Structures in the European Union and Beyond.* 55 (2013): 234–250.

[304] Barbu, A-D., N. Griffiths, and G. Morton. "Achieving Energy Efficiency through Behaviour Change: What Does It Take?" Technical report. EEA (European Environment Agency), April 2013.

[305] This is a controversial topic but there seems to be little doubt that a vegetarian or vegan diet has around half the carbon footprint of a meat diet. In April 2016 the Danish Council of Ethics even recommended a tax on beef, with a view to extending the regulation to all red meats in future.

[306] http://www.worldwildlife.org/industries/dairy

[307] Bridger, Rose. *Plane Truth: Aviation's Real Impact on People and the Environment*. London, UK: Pluto Press, 2013.

[308] Anon. "Air and Rail: Setting the Record Straight (environment, Investment, Mobility and Political Bias)." European Regions Airline Association, 2012.

[309] Druckman, A., Buck, I., Hayward, B., and Jackson, T. "Time, Gender and Carbon: A Study of the Carbon Implications of British Adults' Use of Time." *Ecological Economics* 84 (2012): 153–63.

[310] https://350.org/

[311] https://secure.avaaz.org/en/

[312] https://www.foe.co.uk/

[313] http://www.campaigncc.org/

[314] http://www.greenpeace.org.uk/

[315] http://www.cat.org.uk/index.html

[316] http://www.prb.org/Publications/Lesson-Plans/HumanPopulation/FutureGrowth.aspx

[317] Anon. "Human Population Growth and Greenhouse Gas Emissions." Population-Health-Environment Policy and Practice Group, Wilson Centre, January 2008.

[318] https://mariestopes.org/

CHAPTER 11

[319] http://www.greatchristianhymns.com/once-every-man.html

[320] https://documents.theccc.org.uk/wp-content/uploads/2016/06/2016-CCC-Progress-Report-Executive-Summary.pdf

[321] https://www.theccc.org.uk/wp-content/uploads/2013/06/CCC-Prog-Rep_Chap1_singles_web_1.pdf

[322] https://www.gov.uk/government/publications/2010-to-2015-government-policy-greenhouse-gas-emissions/2010-to-2015-government-policy-greenhouse-gas-emissions

[323] http://www.blog.clientearth.org/climate-change-act-clause-80-can-iron-weaknesses-out/

[324] https://www.gov.uk/government/uploads/system/uploads/attachment_data/file/542558/Consumption_emissions_May16_Final.pdf. Figure 1.

[325] Hopkins, R. *The Transition Handbook (From Oil Dependency to Local Resilience)*. Totnes, UK: Green Books Ltd., 2009.

[326] https://store2123116.ecwid.com/#!/Low-Carbon-Diet-A-30-Day-Program-to-Lose-5000-Pounds/p/21888018/category=5242520

[327] http://www.winacc.org.uk/news/2015-11-19/news-release-cool-communities-programme-launches

[328] von Borgstede, C., M. Andersson, and F. Johnsson. "Public Attitudes to Climate Change and Carbon mitigation—Implications for Energy-Associated Behaviours." *Energy Policy* 57 (2013), 182-193. Quotation after Schwartz (1977), *Advances in Experimental Social Psychology*, vol. 10. Academic Press, New York, pp. 221–279.

[329] Gladwell, Malcolm. *The Tipping Point*. Abacus, 2000.

[330] Bridger, Rose. *Plane Truth: Aviations Real Impact on People and the Environment*. London, UK: Pluto Press, 2013.

[331] Downing, Phil, and Ballantyne, Joe. "Tipping point or turning point? Social marketing & climate change." London, UK: Ipsos MORI Social Research Institute, 2007.

[332] https://www.atmosfair.de/en/klimagerechtigkeit

[333] Garvey, James. *The Persuaders: The Hidden Industry That Wants to Change Your Mind*. London, UK: Icon Books Ltd., 2016.

[334] Francis, Pope. "Encyclical letter Laudato Si' of the holy father Francis, on care for our common home," June 2015. http://w2.vatican.va/content/francesco/en/encyclicals/documents/papa-francesco_20150524_enciclica-laudato-si.html.

[335] *The End of Nature*, Bill McKibben, pp.248, Bloomsbury, second edition 2003.

78309339R00132

Made in the USA
Columbia, SC
14 October 2017